How Two Pray: A Guided Prayer Devotional for Couples, Volume 1
September 2024

How Two Pray: A Guided Prayer Devotional for Couples is a Discovering Family International Publication

Copyright © 2024 by Dr. Harold L. Arnold Jr. and Dalia Ward Arnold
email: harold@haroldarnold.com

ALL RIGHTS RESERVED

Authors: Dr. Harold L. Arnold, Jr and Dalia Ward Arnold
Editor: Melissa Peitch
Cover: Fariha Andleeb

How Two Pray is under copyright protection. No part of this book may be used or reproduced in any manner whatsoever without written permission except in the case of brief quotations embodied in critical articles and reviews. Printed in the United States of America. All rights reserved.

Unless otherwise noted, all Scripture quotations are taken from The Holy Bible, English Standard Version® (ESV®) Copyright © 2001 by Crossway, a publishing ministry of Good News Publishers. All rights reserved.

Quotations marked MSG are from THE MESSAGE, copyright © 1993, 2002, 2018 by Eugene H. Peterson. Used by permission of NavPress. All rights reserved. Represented by Tyndale House Publishers, Inc.

Quotations marked NLT are from the Holy Bible, New Living Translation, copyright ©1996, 2004, 2015 by Tyndale House Foundation. Used by permission of Tyndale House Publishers, Inc., Carol Stream, Illinois 60188. All rights reserved.

Quotations marked NASB are from the New American Standard Bible®, Copyright © 1960, 1971, 1977, 1995, 2020 by The Lockman Foundation. All rights reserved

ISBN: 979-8-9915235-0-9

Printed in the United States of America

DEDICATION

This book is dedicated to the beautiful memory of Dalia's mother, Maria T. Ward, who was the first to believe in who we could be as a couple. Your beauty, inside and out, is forever a part of our origin story. You've inspired us to do our best to be who you believed.

TABLE OF CONTENTS

Introduction

Prayer Lesson 1:   Pray for a Spiritual Discipline in Marriage   1

Prayer Lesson 2:   Pray for a Spiritual Revival in Your Home   10

Prayer Lesson 3:   Pray for Holiness   19

Prayer Lesson 4:   Pray for a Christ-Anchored Marriage   27

Prayer Lesson 5:   Pray for Divine Favor   34

Prayer Lesson 6:   Pray for a Spirit-filled Marital Agenda   42

Prayer Lesson 7:   Pray for Confidence in God's Promises   50

Prayer Lesson 8:   Pray for Godly Discipline   59

Prayer Lesson 9:   Pray for Presence Together   67

Prayer Lesson 10:   Pray for Abundance Through Alignment   76

Prayer Lesson 11:   Pray for Your Delight in the Lord   83

Prayer Lesson 12:   Pray for Agape Love   91

Prayer Lesson 13:   Pray for Graceful Influence   100

Prayer Lesson 14:   Pray for Self-Denial   108

Prayer Lesson 15:   Pray for Preparedness for Spiritual Warfare   115

Prayer Lesson 16:   Pray for Selfless Love   123

Prayer Lesson 17:   Pray for Marital Wisdom   131

APPENDIX: Index of Prayer Needs   139

About the Authors   143

ADVANCED PRAISE FOR
HOW TWO PRAY-VOLUME 1

The Arnold's *How Two Pray* truly speaks to the soul of marriage, and guides us through an introspective journey in discovering what makes a marriage substantive. My wife and I gleaned great wisdom from the "Pray for spiritual discipline" devotional. Upon reading it, we came away enlightened and empowered to examine the faulty assumptions and apathy that often undergird marriage relationships, and how to attack those assumptions in ways that counter relationship stagnation and complacency.
— **GENE & MARSHA REDD, THE MARRIAGE MENTORING NETWORK**

How Two Pray is a captivating devotional every Christian couple should turn to consistently as a highly valuable resource to elevate their marriage. Throughout this Spirit-led transformational book the Arnolds share insightful and impactful stories. What makes this devotional so unique is that the stories about their marriage are honest and transparent… flaws and all, and powerfully illustrate the need to invite the Holy Spirit to be present in order to overcome the challenges of marriage.
—**DICK & JOANN BRUSO, HEARD ABOVE THE NOISE**

I must confess that the Arnolds are courageous and boldly deal with how we live our marriage. This work is not a typical book on marriage as the authors, step by step, gracefully guide us through the most enduring task out of the ordinary life of our marriage. It will require husbands to demonstrate greater care for their wives than their own bodies; and the respect that wives should show their husbands transcends a mere 'submission'. The two shall become "one flesh" is a lifetime process which demands sacrifice and commitment. The Arnolds argue that to pursue such an ideal together is worth a living.
—**DR. ABRAHAM LINCOLN, PASTOR EMERITUS, THE UNIVERSITY BIBLE FELLOWSHIP CHURCH**

Once again Dr. Harold and Dalia have developed a tool that is specially designed to help struggling marriages find solutions and good marriages reach deeper levels of intimacy. Of the many stories in this book, the bicycle story painted a vivid picture to which Kamili and I can relate. In marriage, we have learned the goal is not to win individually or to out perform the other but rather to grow together at the same progressive pace with the goal of crossing the finish line together.
—**PASTOR JONATHAN & KAMILI LEATH, CO-LEADERS, CONVERGE CHURCH**

INTRODUCTION

**CHAINS DO NOT HOLD A MARRIAGE TOGETHER. IT IS THREADS, HUNDREDS OF TINY THREADS, WHICH SEW PEOPLE TOGETHER THROUGH THE YEARS.
—SIMONE SIGNARET**

Marriage is, above all else, a divine relationship with God. For those called to this sacrament, marriage is a Christ-centered path towards righteousness—one intended to remind us of the redemptive and Kingdom-focused work of Christ until the Groom comes again for His Bride, the Church. Within the Kingdom of God, marriage is a righteous journey because it serves three eternal purposes: personal sanctification, relational multiplication, and God-directed glorification.

Kingdom marriage is a miracle. Two sin-prone and deeply flawed individuals join together in a covenant relationship that redirects their worship from self to God. The miracle of Kingdom marriage is that two flawed spouses (who by nature are committed to self-serving gratification) choose instead, through a journey of spiritual formation, to sacrifice their own desires so that Christ is glorified.

Kingdom marriage is spiritual formation. For the Christian, spiritual formation is the process of being conformed to the image of Christ for the glory of God and for the sake of others (2 Corinthians 3:17-18). Literature abounds on the tenets of spiritual formation such as fasting, meditation, silence, solitude and other actions that chip away at sin's grasp on the human soul. But, the most central of all spiritual disciplines is prayer—a reciprocal communication channel that invites God's presence into every aspect of our daily lives (relational, financial, emotional, etc) as a couple. Unfortunately, however, only 11% of married couples ever learn how to pray to God together daily[1] —which involves more than praying before a meal or when some crisis emerges.

The consequences speak for themselves. Repeated studies have shown significantly lower levels of relational trust among couples who fail to pray together. In fact, studies have concluded that shared prayer is the single most powerful predictor of relationship quality across multiple ethnic groups[2]. Other studies have shown greater levels of forgiveness, trust, and unity with decreased infidelity when couples pray for one another (e.g., intercessory prayer). Still other research shows that praying couples experience less anger and frustration, and better self-soothing and conflict resolution practices[3]. One researcher, Dr. W. Bradford Wilcox, explains that "prayer helps couples deal with stress, enables them to focus on shared beliefs and hopes for the future, and allows them to deal constructively with challenges and problems in their relationship and in their lives."

Scholars hypothesize that a couple's prayer life strengthens a "gravitational pull" towards each other as they usher in God's presence and communicate with Him together. Through prayer, God effectively serves as their marriage advocate[4]. The presence of the Holy Spirit is not only the advocate, but the mediator as we let Him lead us to unity as only He can. Less than 1% of couples experience marriage failure when they practice a daily habit of prayer for God's resources, wisdom, and protection[5]. The miracle of Kingdom marriage is daily and spiritually formative prayer.

The hypotheses of contemporary research, however, only validate what Jesus' brother James recorded more than two millennia ago: "Make this your common practice: Confess your sins to each other and pray for each other so that you can live together whole and healed" (James 5:16). Godly relationships (of which marriage is a foundational example) that are whole and healed are powered by confession and prayer. Without a consistent prayer life, couples not only suffer in fractured marriages but they also lack the anointing and divine power to obliterate the strongholds of the Adversary, to command healing of illnesses in the name of Christ, and to evangelize salvation and sanctification to a lost and dying world. While the sincere prayers of any individual touch the heart of God, the prayers of a covenant couple wield a special anointing.

Our charge then as Christian couples is not just to pray but to learn how to pray together—identified in this book, *How Two Pray*.

"Teach us to pray" was the insightful request of one of Jesus' disciples (Luke 11:1) as Jesus concluded His prayers in a certain unnamed place. Jesus' response to this simple request, ceremonially dubbed 'The Lord's Prayer,' has guided His followers' prayer protocol for more than two thousand years. As His disciples, being in the presence of Jesus is extraordinary. But, as sin-laden couples faced with the demanding stressors of life, we must do better than 11% of us praying together regularly.

Our hope is that this book serves as a reliable, Spirit-inspired guide to your regular communication with God as a couple and an open invitation for God to be your marital advocate.

Our Testimony of Spiritual Formation in Marriage

We have been married for well over three decades. For all of those years, we have proclaimed Christ as our Lord and Savior. We have been regular attendees and tithers at our local church, and held a variety of ministry leadership positions over the years. Yet, for most of these years, we have not had a great marriage. As a husband, I (Harold) was far too selfish, analytical, and ultimately inconsiderate of Dalia's needs. Most, though certainly not all, of the mediocrity of our marriage is a result of my insensitivity to the spiritual needs of my wife.

As a wife, Dalia also highlights her own struggles with selfishness, pride and impatience. Dalia describes being so focused on getting things her way that she did not seek the Lord on how to bring out the best in Harold. Gratefully, she now continues to mature in the knowledge that God's way of loving, forgiving and showing grace is a win for the both of us.

Like most couples, we brought a lot of psychological baggage into our marriage at the tender age of twenty-two years old. Our personalities are so extremely different that many negative triggers appeared around each corner. Despite all of our strengths, there are only two things that saved our marriage. First, as Christians, we strongly oppose divorce based on our understanding of scripture. As such, we would have only considered it under the most heinous of circumstances. So, it is unlikely that we would ever have legally divorced. But, what could have realistically happened was an emotional separation. The second element that saved our marriage was prayer. For our entire marriage, we have prayed together practically every day. Through good and bad times, we prayed together. When we were joyful or upset with each other, we prayed together.

Then, we hit some crisis points in our marriage where it was clear that praying together was not enough. The Holy Spirit showed us that we needed to expand this into prayer and devotions as a couple. Over the past several years, we embarked on a mission to be more intentional in a spiritually formative practice of daily devotion and prayer together. The results have been astounding. Our love and trust in each other has grown exponentially. We have become more unified in our vision and goal setting. We have learned to genuinely care for and nurture one another. We rarely, if ever, try to win or persuade the other to one point of view. We have matured in many ways to wait for God's timing and desires to be revealed. This mutual trust and reciprocal decision-making enables us to lead a fledgling but Spirit-led non-profit called Eusebeia, with a mission to lead a spiritual revival for Christian marriage. Each year the ranks of Eusebeia grow larger as more couples are drawn to this vision of a spiritual revival in their own marriage.

Without question, we have a long way to grow as a couple in pursuit of Christlikeness. As an organization, Eusebeia's goal for one thousand Christian couples united in a Spirit-led revival still feels far off. Yet, there is one thing that makes us confident that we are becoming the Kingdom marriage and ministry that God intends—our commitment to spiritually formative prayer and devotions together. This book is born of our years-long (and ongoing) journey to discover the best version of our marriage, the way God designed it to be from the foundation of the earth.

Our prayer is that this book will awaken the giant within every Christian couple that opens its pages. We pray for the abundance of humility, grace, and thanksgiving that you will need to consistently invest in your own journey of prayer and devotion. We can promise you that what you discover on the other side of this investment is a glimpse into the marriage that you have always dreamed was possible. You will, without question, face resistance and disappointments on this journey. Just remember that as long as you keep going and continuously submit your challenges to God together, your marriage wins, and God is glorified. Ultimately, that is all that matters.

1. https://www.encompasscc.org/blog/an-amazing-secret-to-marriage-success
2. "The Couple That Prays Together. Race and Ethnicity, Religion, and Relationship Quality Among Working-Age Adults" Journal of Marriage and Family, Ellison, Burdette, Wilcox, Journal of Marriage and Family 72 (August 2010): 963 – 975
3. https://ifstudies.org/blog/when-religious-couples-pray
4. https://www.focusonthefamily.com/marriage/what-research-says-about-couples-who-pray-together/
5. A 1997 Gallup Poll done by the National Association of Marriage Enhancement (nameonline.net)

HOW TO USE THIS COUPLES DEVOTIONAL

BOOK STRUCTURE

This book is designed for flexibility on your prayer journey as a couple. The key to growth with this book is to find a rhythm that you can sustain together. This book is volume 1 of 3, which in total comprises 52 prayer lessons—one for each week of the year. Each prayer lesson is comprised of six parts:

- Biblical Scripture (memory verse to rehearse while engaging the lesson)
- Breath Prayer (short prayer to utter as you navigate your daily routine)
- Object Story (focal marriage enrichment lesson)
- Let's Talk (two daily questions to facilitate couple sharing)
- Let's Reflect (integrative task to apply the prayer lesson for marital growth)
- Let's Pray (five daily prayers that can be read together)

The centerpiece of each weekly lesson is the Object Story. Storytelling is integral to the human experience as the Lord in His infinite wisdom designed us to live and imagine our history through stories. Apple founder and visionary Steve Jobs may have said it best in his often-cited quote, "The most powerful person in the world is the storyteller. The storyteller sets the vision, values and agenda of an entire generation that is to come."

Stories are central to this prayer devotional because they capture the dynamics that we face as we go through the daily vicissitudes of marriage. These stories are told in a way to imprint these ideas and imagery on your conscious and subconscious selves.

Through these devotionals, you will encounter everyday stories of socks, bicycles, fences, and so much more. These Object Stories are raw, personal experiences captured over the past three years as we navigated the issues that most couples must traverse sooner or later to one degree or another. These stories are real and we have done our best to present them authentically as they transpired, while also offering a spiritual and biblical overlay that matured (or should have matured) our marriage. Our prayer is that you will see yourselves in our stories.

More importantly, our belief is that Christ is going to meet you in the reading and sharing of these stories. We strongly encourage you to take the few minutes to read the Object Story together aloud. In full transparency, as you navigate these stories, questions, and guided prayers, the Holy Spirit is going to ask more of you. But, even as He asks more of you, He will expand your capacity as stewards of your Kingdom marriage. Your marriage is about to elevate beyond what you thought possible. Such is the power of Spirit-led stories.

There are many ways for you to utilize this book to grow your marriage. Frankly, you will grow as a couple as long as you are consistently sharing together and inviting the Holy Spirit to be present with you. Your growth is a byproduct of your consistent deference to the Holy Spirit. It is not the words you read or pray. The habit you establish in meeting with Him is the means for your transformation. This book is simply a guide to reinforce that habit. Here are three suggestions to use this guide, depending how much time you want to dedicate to the spiritual growth of your marriage.

METHOD 1: SPIRITUAL IMMERSION

The goal of the Spiritual Immersion method is to intensify the spiritual and emotional connection of your marriage by navigating one full lesson each week. If done each week, the fifty-two prayer lessons will take you through an entire calendar year. At the beginning of each week, perhaps each Sunday, read the Biblical Scripture and Breath Prayer together. Strive to commit the Breath Prayer and/or the Biblical Scripture to memory. Write the Breath Prayer on an index card that you carry with you so that you can recite it throughout the day—practicing what the Apostle Paul describes as "praying without ceasing" (1 Thessalonians 5:17). At the beginning of each week, read the Object Story and discuss what you each take away for your marriage. Pause and allow the Holy Spirit to speak to each of you. Each weekday, choose one or two Let's Talk Prompts and share your responses with each other. Read aloud the Let's Pray for each weekday together. Whenever you have time during the week, spend some time completing the Let's Reflect Activity and sharing what it has meant to you.

METHOD 2: SPIRITUAL INTERCESSION

The goal of the Spiritual Intercession method is to expand the prayer coverage of your marriage by referencing the index of marital challenges at the end of this book and selecting a topic or struggle that you both feel is in need of healing or growth. Each growth area has one or more Prayer Lessons that may enrich your relationship. For each lesson, spend as much time as necessary reading and memorizing the Biblical Scripture and the Breath Prayer. Slowly read through the Object Story together as a couple—possibly reading it multiple times over the course of a week. Each weekday, thoroughly discuss both questions as much as your available time allows. On the weekend, spend some time completing the Let's Reflect Activity and sharing what it has meant to you to complete it.

Given this is a growth area for you, do not feel rushed. It may be advantageous to spend multiple weeks on one Prayer Lesson. After you have completed all of the lesson components, discuss how your marriage has been transformed by the commitment. After you have thoroughly completed one Prayer Lesson, proceed to any others that are associated with this area of need and repeat the process.

METHOD 3: SPIRITUAL INDUCTION

The Spiritual Induction method is for couples who do not habitually engage in either insightful conversation or spiritually enrichment activities as a couple. The goal of the Spiritual Induction method is to establish a routine of engagement as a couple through a process of incremental engagement that allows the establishment of a habit. This incremental approach is divided into four cycles:

- For the first three-month cycle, proceed serially through the Prayer Lessons with focus on a minimum of two sections each weekday—the Object Story and the daily prayer. At the beginning of the week, read the Object Story together and recite the daily prayer each weekday. You may incorporate other sections at your discretion.
- For the second three-month cycle, add at least one of the daily questions to your daily routine. Again, feel free to incorporate other sections at your discretion.
- For the third three-month cycle, add recitation of the Breath Prayer throughout your daily routine. Check in with each other at the end of each day and see how the Breath Prayer impacted you.
- For the fourth three-month period, add the Let's Reflect Activity to your routine as a weekend activity.
- By the end of twelve months, you will have established a formidable prayer routine as a couple.

Now, as a couple, choose the method that feels accessible today for where you are in your own spiritual maturity as a couple. Do not be overly ambitious. The most important thing to do is a little more than you are doing today. Then, keep increasing your commitment as the routine becomes more familiar. Our prayers are with you as you learn how two pray.

PRAY FOR SPIRITUAL DISCIPLINE IN MARRIAGE

REFERENCE SCRIPTURE

"For this reason I remind you to fan into flame the gift of God, which is in you through the laying on of my hands. For the Spirit God gave us does not make us timid, but gives us power, love and self-discipline."
—2 Timothy 1:6-7, ESV.

BREATH PRAYER

Through our understanding and practice of the spiritual disciplines, show us as a couple how to surrender our control to you.

OBJECT STORY

DISCIPLINE MAKES A GOOD MARRIAGE GREAT

On July 16, 1999, John F. Kennedy Jr., son of US President John F. Kennedy, took off from Essex County airport in New Jersey in his single-engine Piper Saratoga, on his way to Martha's Vineyard with his wife and sister-in-law. As a relatively inexperienced pilot, Kennedy was ill-prepared for what he would face on a hazy, moonless night. He crashed the plane, killing all on board. In its final report released in 2000, the National Transportation Safety Board concluded that the crash was caused by an inexperienced pilot who became disoriented in the dark and lost control of the plane—plummeting from 2200 feet to 1100 feet in a span of 14 seconds and then disappearing from radar.

Beginning this first lesson with such a tragic account feels like a strange way to start; unfortunately, far too many Christian couples have also 'lost control' of their marriage and crashed. There are important marriage lessons that we can glean from the heartbreaking experience of JFK Jr.

First, an experienced flight instructor had offered to accompany them that fateful night. Kennedy declined, preferring to do it alone. In my experience as a marriage educator, I (Harold) have watched far too many Christian couples try to do marriage alone. They underestimate how challenging it can be to navigate the rough spots alone. We all need community to be our best selves as a Kingdom couple. It is pride that comes before a fall (Proverbs 16:18). Second, experts' reconstruction of JFK Jr.'s piloting has a clear and simple explanation of why the crash happened: his plane was caught in a spiral dive that requires the pilot to rely solely on their flight instrumentation rather than what they can sense.

Prayer Lesson 1
Pray for Spiritual Discipline in Marriage　　　　　　　　　2 Timothy 1:6-7

The disturbing irony of a spiral dive is that inside the plane everything "feels" completely normal—the pilot thinks he or she is flying with the wings level. Given his inexperience, JFK Jr. had no idea they were mere seconds from death.

How many Christian couples have no idea how close their marriage is to its own death? Unpredictability and challenges tend to reveal cracks in the marriage—selfishness, stubbornness, pride. But, these couples are caught in their own proverbial spiral dive when it comes to their marriage. They feel like things are fine; in reality, the marriage is dying.

"We must face the fact that many today are notoriously careless in their living. This attitude finds its way into the church. We have liberty, we have money, we live in comparative luxury. As a result, discipline practically has disappeared. What would a violin solo sound like if the strings on the musician's instrument were all hanging loose, not stretched tight, not 'disciplined'?" —A. W. Tozer

When we are going through difficult situations, the Lord is often calling us to discipline. While I certainly do not fully know where God intends to take us in this journey, He has directed us to the final words of the Apostle Paul to Timothy: "For this reason I remind you to fan into flame the gift of God, which is in you through the laying on of my hands. For the Spirit God gave us does not make us timid, but gives us power, love and self-discipline" (2 Timothy 1:6-7).

Will you join us on this road to discipline? Personally, I have thought of myself as a disciplined person. It has been part of my identity. However, the Lord is showing me many ways in which I am very spiritually undisciplined.

It is sobering and humbling to see just how far I actually am from the discipline to which God calls me. And there have been consequences. This lack of spiritual discipline places an inordinate strain on my marriage, my health, my stress level, and my creativity. God is calling me to the spiritual disciplines to grow my dependence on Him, to grow my courage, and to show how far His power can extend through me as I mature.

We are again reminded of Tozer's warning that 'discipline practically has disappeared' in the church. Yet, the spiritual revival of your marriage and mine depends wholly on these spiritual disciplines. Let us not make the same mistakes of JFK Jr. on that fateful night more than a decade ago. Don't try to do marriage alone and don't let the Adversary (or your emotions or pride) tell you that 'everything is fine.' It isn't. How will this year stand out in your marriage? We pray that your year ahead will be remembered as the year discipline made a 'good' or 'fine' marriage great.

Prayer Lesson 1
Pray for Spiritual Discipline in Marriage

2 Timothy 1:6-7

Let's Talk

MONDAY
- What, if any, parallels can you draw from JFK Jr.'s piloting errors as compared to the missteps you each have made in your marriage?
- The danger and travesty of a spiral dive in an aircraft is that everything feels normal to the pilot though s/he is seconds from catastrophe. Are there ways in which your marriage is closer to emotional calamity than you realize?

TUESDAY
- What steps do you take as a couple to consider and conform to Christ in your interactions with one another?
- In what, if any, ways do you take each other for granted?

WEDNESDAY
- What type of attention does your spouse most enjoy from you?
- What, if any, spiritual disciplines do you regularly practice in your marriage? How does this impact the way you walk together as a couple?

THURSDAY
- What aspects of your different personalities make consistent practice of spiritual disciplines more easy or more challenging together as a couple?
- What and how much are you willing to sacrifice of yourself for this year to be the most extraordinary year of your marriage to date?

FRIDAY
- What evidence do you see that your marriage has room for improvement?
- What has God already invested in your marriage that can help you grow?

2 Timothy 1:6-7

Prayer Lesson 1
Pray for Spiritual Discipline in Marriage

Let's Reflect

> Pray for Spiritual Discipline in Marriage

This week, your reflections and prayers focus on the faulty assumptions and apathy that erode your marriage over time. Take a few minutes to write down some of the poor assumptions that weigh down your marriage. From where did these assumptions come? Brainstorm and record 2-3 commitments that you are willing to make as an offering to the Lord to grow yourself and your marriage over the course of this year.

_____

_____

_____

_____

_____

_____

_____

Prayer Lesson 1
Pray for Spiritual Discipline in Marriage 2 Timothy 1:6-7

Let's Pray

MONDAY

Dear Lord, we admit that there are times that we have been overconfident in our ability to carry our marriages in our own strength rather than depending on your divine instrumentation—the Word of God. This self-sufficiency has been insufficient and has often put our marriage in a dark and disoriented place. We say things we know we shouldn't say. We behave in ways of which we are not proud. We are too prideful for our own good. We repent for all those times when we tried to fly this plane of marriage without relying on the navigational abilities of the Holy Spirit. Forgive us for our haughty and self-righteous attitudes. This year we want to renounce these flaws in our marriage and heal the fissures that have divided us. We have always needed you. But, thank you for helping us to realize the depth of that need before it is too late. In the name of the Absolute Jesus Christ of Nazareth we pray. Amen.

TUESDAY

Dear Lord, it's easy to become complacent in marriage. The romantic attention that we doled out to each other has long faded. The busyness of jobs, kids, and other responsibilities has weakened our focus on one another. Romantic feelings are fleeting when they aren't cultivated in the love of Christ—a love which always perseveres, always sacrifices, and always points us to God the Father. Help us to fall deeper in love with you so that we can deepen the love in our marriage. We pray for a spirit of attentiveness in our marriage so that we never again take each other for granted. And, in the instances when we slip, we pray that the grace that you show us will help us show grace for growth to each other. In the name of the Absolute Jesus Christ of Nazareth we pray. Amen.

WEDNESDAY

Dear Lord, thank you for paying attention to every aspect of our lives. When we go through tough stretches, we can remain confident that the difficulty isn't because you've lost sight of us. Often, the difficulty is a result of your attentiveness to our growth and maturity in our Christian walk and in our marriage. In our humanity, we crave attention. We fear isolation and loneliness more than almost anything else. Feelings of rejection can paralyze us. But, you teach us that you will never leave us or forsake us (Deuteronomy 31:8). You never stop paying attention to the state of our soul—putting us in situations where we must trust in your divine presence and power. We often thank you for forgiving us for our sins. But, today, we also want to share our gratitude for never forgetting us. In the name of the Absolute Jesus Christ of Nazareth we pray. Amen.

THURSDAY

Dear Lord, you are the same yesterday, today, and forever. You are an unchanging God and we can depend on you. The challenge is that as husband and wife, we are constantly being influenced in negative ways by our culture. The expectations we have for each other vacillate from week to week depending on our mood. The satisfaction that we feel with each other's efforts in this marriage depends on those expectations. There is very little that is guaranteed and predictable about our marriage. Help us to remember that you are steadfast, and our marriage will be stable if we depend on you and trust in you above all. In the name of the Absolute Jesus Christ of Nazareth we pray. Amen.

FRIDAY

Dear Lord, we feel convicted by the words of A. W. Tozer that "discipline has practically disappeared from the church," being replaced by convenience, comfort, and mediocrity. Contemplative reading and worship have been usurped by feel-good platitudes. Conviction of sin has been pushed aside in favor of focus solely on grace for the sinner.

Prayer Lesson 1
Pray for Spiritual Discipline in Marriage 2 Timothy 1:6-7

The pursuit of Christlikeness has given way to the pursuit of 'spiritual' enlightenment. The undaunted commitment to the words and actions of Jesus Christ is de-prioritized in favor of selective pursuits that fit the Christian narrative of our culture. We have strayed far from you, Lord. We repent of our disobedience and commit to discipline, so that our marriage can be lived in a manner that is acceptable in your sight. In the name of the Absolute Jesus Christ of Nazareth we pray. Amen.

PRAY FOR A SPIRITUAL REVIVAL IN YOUR HOME

REFERENCE SCRIPTURE

"Here is another thing you do. You cover the Lord's altar with tears, weeping and groaning because he pays no attention to your offerings and doesn't accept them with pleasure... I'll tell you why! Because the Lord witnessed the vows you and your wife made when you were young. But, you have been unfaithful to her, though she remained your faithful partner, the wife of your marriage vows."—Malachi 2:13-14, NLT.

BREATH PRAYER

Bless our marriage to be the spiritual fortress of our home and a model of security to our community.

OBJECT STORY

MARRIAGE IN THE HANDS OF AN ANGRY GOD

On July 8th, 1741, one of Christianity's most renowned preachers, Jonathan Edwards, took the pulpit in Enfield, Connecticut to deliver what is arguably the most famous sermon ever preached on American soil, "Sinners in the Hands of an Angry God." This heated sermon is widely regarded as one of the main catalysts for what would become known as The Great Awakening—an unprecedented series of revivals across Britain and the thirteen colonies that convicted the spiritual consciousness of a young America and forever changed the trajectory of the Church and the Christian faith. When evaluating the calamities of our current time, they evoke a question. Are we yet again in the hands of an angry God? Could the dour and recalcitrant state of our Christian marriages be, at least partially, to blame? On both questions, my belief is "Yes."

On May 15, 2022, an 18-year-old walked into a grocery store in Buffalo and killed 13 people (11 of them Black). By his own admission he targeted Buffalo because it was the city with the most Black residents in closest proximity to his home. Erie County sheriff John Garcia called the massacre "pure evil."

Just ten days later on May 25, another 18-year-old shot his own grandmother and then proceeded to Robb Elementary School clad in body armor and armed with an AR-15 rifle and high-capacity magazine. Before his ill-fated rampage was over, 19 small children lay dead along with the gunman.

Then again five days later (May 30), police arrested a 16-year-old who was secretly recruiting other high school students to carry out a mass shooting at their high school in Berkeley, California. A search of his home uncovered assault rifles, several knives, and sundry parts to create explosive devices.

Across this great nation, most Americans proclaim outrage and question, "How could this happen?" We somehow feel that—if we can blame a listless Congress, powerful lobbies, or hate groups—we can somehow limit, if not eradicate, such "pure evil". While there is an element of truth in the culpability of each of these entities, the Truth is not in our culture's convenient but short-sighted rhetoric. The Truth is much more complex, personal, and convicting. How much of America's "pure evil" falls at the feet of the Church? How much responsibility lies with me?

As I (Harold) sat thinking about the violence, hate, and rampant disregard for human life, the Spirit led me to the book of Malachi chapter 2 for the Lord's warning to His people. I can't overemphasize the point that this Word is directed to God's people. "I [The Lord] will bring a terrible curse against you. I will curse even the blessings you receive... I will punish your descendants." Our children are our greatest blessings. But, what does the Lord mean that our blessings will be cursed and our descendants will be punished? Are we in the hands of an angry God?

How is Satan able to corrupt young minds such that teenagers transform into "pure evil" killing machines? How does the Adversary distort sensibilities such that hate becomes indiscriminate and nothing is sacred or immune—not even churches or elementary schools? The answer is hidden in plain sight. Satan is fighting a spiritual battle—intent to steal, kill, and destroy.

Prayer Lesson 2
Pray for a Spiritual Revival in Your Home Malachi 2:13-14

The sad reality is that many children, even those in Christian homes, are growing up in spiritually fractured homes; this corruption has left many children spiritually (and often physically) unprotected. We must stop the petty marital bickering and implore the Holy Spirit to make our marriages worthy of another Great Awakening. Uncompromising worship and stewardship of the Lord's resources is the only path towards blessings that are not cursed. As Christian couples, we must stop depending only on our culture's carnal weapons. We must turn from our unfaithful ways—selfishness, materialism, and apathy. We must unite in our faith and in our prayers. We must become unified spiritual bedrocks in our homes. And, we must take the time to spiritually invest in our children, in our homes, churches, and neighborhoods. Even in the hands of an angry God, our marriages can become lightning rods of revival as we pray for national healing of hearts and minds.

Let's Talk

MONDAY
- In what ways do you see warnings of God's anger in the lives of people around you—at work, in the neighborhood, and at church?
- What attitudes and patterns of behavior do you observe around you that stokes the ire of God?

TUESDAY
- As you look around the perimeter of your circle of family and friends, what evidences do you see of brokenness in relationships between family members, friendships, and God?
- When you reflect back a couple of generations, what patterns of emotional, financial, and spiritual brokenness do you see in your family of origin? How does this make you feel?

WEDNESDAY
- In Malachi 2:13-14, scripture directly associates the troubles of life with the lack of faithfulness in marriage. In what areas is your lack of faithfulness to God in your marriage stifling God's blessings to your home?
- What unanswered prayers have you been offering to God? How might your own disobedience to God as a couple be hindering your prayers?

THURSDAY
- With what resources has the Lord blessed you, that He is calling you to be better stewards of as a couple?
- What do you each need to do to be a more righteous steward of God's resources to you?

FRIDAY
- God blesses you to be a blessing. Beyond your own immediate family, to whom is God calling your marriage to be a blessing?
- In whose lives and in what ways do you see God already moving? Accept this as a spiritual invitation to join as a couple in supporting God's work in someone else.

Prayer Lesson 2
Pray for a Spiritual Revival in Your Home

Malachi 2:13-14

Let's Reflect

> Pray for a Spiritual Revival in Your Home

This week focuses on the myriad ways that sinfulness invades our culture and our homes. As you reflect on this week's lesson and questions, consider the ways in which your marriage has both pleased and angered God. In the space below, record practical ways that as a couple you can show more gratitude and generosity to God, towards one another, and to others.

_____

_____

_____

_____

_____

_____

_____

Let's Pray

MONDAY

Dear Lord, your prophet Isaiah cried out to you that he is a man of unclean lips and that he dwells in the midst of a people of unclean lips (Isaiah 6:5). What was true of Isaiah is true of us as well. When we compare our spiritual depravity with the standard that Christ set for us, we feel a sense of shame and conviction. We know better than we are behaving. Too often, we forget the price that you paid for us. Grace is not cheap. Just as you took the iniquity and sinfulness away from your servant Isaiah, we ask that you give us a repentant and clean heart so that our marriage is pleasing unto you. In the name of the Absolute Jesus Christ of Nazareth we pray. Amen.

TUESDAY

Dear Lord, when we look at the history of your children, we see how you bless them when they turn from wickedness and idolatry to worship you alone. But, we also see how destruction follows their disobedience. We see the evidence of this destruction in our own culture and homes. But, we are encouraged that scripture shows when your children abandon our wickedness and pray to you that you hear our cries. You will heal our land and our families. We ask today that your healing rain wash over our family. Let our marriage be the agent for transformation in our extended family and neighborhood. In the name of the Absolute Jesus Christ of Nazareth we pray. Amen.

WEDNESDAY

Dear Lord, we have seen your blessings with our own eyes and our inner spirit has been enlivened by the power of your Holy Spirit. But, we've also experienced seasons in a spiritual desert as a couple—times when you felt distant. We know you have not withdrawn from us. But, we have distanced ourselves from you because of the ways our marriage has not been faithful to your Word. Our innermost desire is that you get the glory from our marriage. We pray for another chance for our marriage to be a light that directs others towards you. May we be the "blameless and innocent, children of God above reproach in the midst of a crooked and perverse population" (Philippians 2:15). In the name of the Absolute Jesus Christ of Nazareth we pray. Amen.

THURSDAY

Dear Lord, when Jesus was preparing His disciples for His earthly departure, He told them a parable about a master who left resources in the hands of his servants for them to invest until his return. You have placed many resources in our hands as a couple. But, we have not been the consistently faithful stewards of these resources that you have called us to be. Forgive us for those times we have buried your resources in the ground and not acted on them. Forgive us for those times we have been distracted from investing what you've given us. We are learning the ways the Adversary distracts us. And, we vow to do better as a couple in multiplying the return on the investment that you have made in our marriage. In the name of the Absolute Jesus Christ of Nazareth we pray. Amen.

FRIDAY

Dear Lord, you are blessing us to be a blessing to our neighbors. Gratitude and generosity are always two spiritual weapons that you have given us to break through spiritual, relational, and financial bondage. Our marriage will be a paragon of gratitude—offering thanks to you each day for your presence in our lives. Our marriage will be an extension of your generosity—giving to others freely just as you continue to give to us. In these ways, our marriage will be a place of your joy not your anger. This joy will be our strength as a couple and be a ministry to all those who witness your power through us. In the name of the Absolute Jesus Christ of Nazareth we pray. Amen.

PRAY FOR HOLINESS

REFERENCE SCRIPTURE

Then the Lord said to him, "Now you Pharisees clean the outside of the cup and of the dish, but inside you are full of greed and wickedness. You fools! Did not the one who made the outside make the inside also? So give for alms those things that are within; and see, everything will be clean for you."—Luke 11:39-41, NIV.

BREATH PRAYER

Through God's grace, may our lifestyle together display purity according to the movement of the Holy Spirit.

OBJECT STORY
IT'S TIME TO CLEAN HOUSE

Harold's mother (Mom Dorothy) was never in the military. But, we tell people all the time that Mom Dorothy would have given most drill sergeants a run for their money in her younger years. When Harold was growing up, Mom Dorothy had a very low tolerance for a dirty house. Under the scrutiny of mom's ever watching eye, the bedsheets needed to be pulled taut. The dirty dishes mustn't remain in the sink too long. The floors should be swept first and then mopped. Here is one detail that speaks for itself: Mom Dorothy would iron underwear! For Mom Dorothy, cleaning was not an occasional process reserved for when company is coming—it was a lifestyle.

When we think about a 'clean' standard for marriage, we think of Mom Dorothy's devotion to a clean house. God sets a high expectation as to how we should live our marriage. God challenges us husbands to love our spouse like He loves the church. He insists that wives show respect for their husbands. The Bible (Ephesians 5:25-31) shows us how this love-respect dynamic is the precursor to the "one flesh" standard to which God holds us. But, this type of love is more than saying, 'I love you.' God's standard of love is for husbands to demonstrate greater care for their wives than for their own bodies. Similarly, the respect that wives should show their husbands transcends the shallow 'submission' upon which most of us focus. Rather, it is empowering his identity and his dreams. This love-respect tandem fosters a sense of oneness that the Apostle Paul dubs a 'profound mystery' that helps us better understand Christ's relationship with the church.The clean standard of Christian marriage is a mysterious and transcendent unity that propels the couple to transform everything in their path.

Prayer Lesson 3
Pray for Holiness

Luke 11:39-41

God wants the sheets of our marriage bed pulled tight. He wants the dust bunnies swept from every corner of our marriage. He wants the marital furniture polished so well that His reflection is clearly seen in them. He even wants us to iron the wrinkles out of the parts of the marriage that others may not see—the 'underwear,' if you will.

Our efforts to meet God's standard for marriage within our human capacity are badly failing. It is not good enough to look good on the outside while excusing yourself of the love and respect needed for a godly marriage. It is not good enough to just aim for a better marriage than what you saw in your own parents. It is not good enough to stay out of divorce court. It is not good enough to have fewer fights than other couples that you know. These are all good things. But, they are not even close to the clean standard that God is asking for your marriage. In far too many instances, our marriages are unacceptable offerings to God with dire consequences noted in Malachi (2:13), "You cover the Lord's altar with tears, with weeping and groaning because he no longer regards the offering or accepts it with favor from your hand."

May we encourage you to look under the bed, in the closets, and in the neglected corners of your marriage and ask yourselves whether there is any aspect of your marriage that is an unacceptable offering to God. Ask God to bring people in your marriage that will encourage purity without compromise. Then, when you know better, do better.

Without question, we all need grace in pursuing this godly standard. However, it always starts with the conviction to pursue God's clean standard with the same dogged zeal that my mother pursued that clean house. In marriage, cleanliness is not for special occasions. Clean is a lifestyle.

Let's Talk

MONDAY
- How important is it to each of you to live in a clean space? How similar or different are your respective standards of "clean"?
- What, if any, connection do you see between the standard of cleanliness you desire for your home as compared to your marriage?

TUESDAY
- What does having a "clean" marriage mean to each of you?
- Is a "clean" marriage something you ever reach or must you settle for pursuing it? Explain your thinking.

WEDNESDAY
- In what situations have you been more concerned with how clean you look on the outside as a couple versus how clean you are on the inside?
- In your mind, what causes you to settle for a less than godly standard of cleanliness in your attitude towards your spouse and marriage?

THURSDAY
- Based on Malachi 2:13, have you ever considered that some of your prayers to the Lord may be hindered because the clean standard in your marriage is neglected?
- How can you overcome the areas of deficit in your marriage and family that Malachi 2:13 is addressing?

FRIDAY
- Who have you invited into your lives to be an example of a "clean" marriage?
- What do you see as the connection between grace and cleanliness in your marriage?

Prayer Lesson 3
Pray for Holiness

Luke 11:39-41

Let's Reflect

> Pray for Holiness

This week your reflections and prayers focus on your commitment to a godly standard of cleanliness and purity in your marriage. In our humanity, we will always stumble in our consistency to this standard. Showing the grace of Christ towards each other is the only way to forgive and keep growing forward. Discuss some ways that you have successfully shown grace to each other in recent days and weeks, as well as grace lapses that you've felt.

_____

_____

_____

_____

_____

_____

_____

Let's Pray

MONDAY

Dear Lord, you are the Living Water. You tell us in the book of John (7:38) that whoever believes in you will have "rivers of living water flow from them". We know that the power of "living water" is that it flows rather than being sedentary and stale. We desire the Holy Spirit in us to flow in a way that our family and friends witness our transformation to be the clean couple that you intended us to be when we stood at the altar in holy matrimony. We can't relive the past, but we can invite the Living Water to cleanse us from all unrighteousness and sin so that you can be glorified through us. In the name of the Absolute Jesus Christ of Nazareth we pray. Amen.

TUESDAY

Dear Lord, we have different styles and opinions on what it would even look like to live a "clean" marriage. But, you give us stories of broken people who found a path to righteous and clean lives through their obedience to you. King David was an adulterer. But, he asked for a clean heart and you describe him as a man after your own heart because he was willing to do your will (1 Samuel 13:14). We certainly have many missteps as a couple. But we are working towards letting the Holy Spirit clean us from the inside through prayer, fasting, scripture reading, fellowship with the saints, and devotions. We want you to describe us the way that you describe David. We want the Lord to say of us, "Here is a couple after my own heart." We want this goal to be the top priority of our lives—more than public accolades, financial gain, and material accomplishments. In the name of the Absolute Jesus Christ of Nazareth we pray. Amen.

WEDNESDAY

Dear Lord, we care so much about how other people see our marriage. Admittedly, to our fault, we pay more attention to how family members, neighbors, and church members see us than to how you see us. Most people think we have everything together as a couple. Some even think of our marriage as a model. The truth is that when we are out of the public eye we are often not kind and gentle. We forget to nurture one another, especially when we disagree about something. We can be slow to extend grace when one of us messes up. Our communication can be tense and sometimes filled with ungodly language. We would not want anyone to see us this way. But, Lord we know that you see us as we truly are. Our only hope is to turn to the Holy Spirit to reform our love for one another by sacrificing our individual wants in service to you. In the name of the Absolute Jesus Christ of Nazareth we pray.

THURSDAY

Dear Lord, we know that you hear us because in your omnipresence nothing happens outside of your awareness. We know that you could do something for us because you are all powerful. We even know that you already know our needs before we even ask because you are all knowing. So, why does it feel like you are ignoring the things that matter most to us when they matter most? We have heard it said that you always answer our prayers with one of three answers—"Yes", "No", or "Not Yet". Even when it disappoints our flesh, we want to be content with whatever answer you give to us. We will worship you in your omnipotence, omnipresence, and omniscience regardless. We may not be there yet. But, we are closer than we were yesterday. In the name of the Absolute Jesus Christ of Nazareth we pray. Amen.

FRIDAY

Dear Lord, it is hard to live a "clean" marriage when we don't have great examples in our lives, especially when we didn't grow up in homes with a strong marriage. We know that marriage grows in vineyards of Christian couples who are constantly fertilizing their marriages. You know our most intimate needs as a couple. Will you send us other couples whom we can walk alongside and grow with? Will you put us in a position of trust with couples that prioritize worshipping you more than the things of this world? Will you help us become the kind of couple in whom mature and clean couples want to invest of themselves? Will you give us the courage to be vulnerable so that we can grow in a community of "clean" couples? Will you give us the strength to stay resilient when we are disappointed by those who don't want to grow with us? What we do know is that accountability and fellowship are your desires for us. So, here we are. Send us. In the name of the Absolute Jesus Christ of Nazareth we pray. Amen.

PRAY FOR A CHRIST-ANCHORED MARRIAGE

REFERENCE SCRIPTURE

"So that by two unchangeable things, in which it is impossible for God to lie, we who have fled for refuge might have strong encouragement to hold fast to the hope set before us. We have this as a sure and steadfast anchor of the soul, a hope that enters into the inner place behind the curtain."—Hebrews 6:18-19, ESV.

BREATH PRAYER

Anchor our hopeful expectation in an abiding trust that you are working all things out for the good of marriage.

OBJECT STORY
IS YOUR MARRIAGE ON THE SHELF?

One evening, we returned home and opened the door to a mess—jackets and caps haphazardly strewn around the mudroom. It took us a few more seconds to figure out what happened.

As we discovered, the entire mudroom closet shelving system had collapsed—taking with it everything that was hanging and sitting on it. Upon closer examination of the damage, I (Harold) saw that the screws had pulled from the drywall. Apparently, the contractor who remodeled our mudroom had not attached the weight-bearing shelf to the wood studs, or even drywall anchors.

This collapsed shelf is a perfect illustration for the struggle that others and we face in marriage. The issue is not the shelf. The issue is the anchors. The issue is not your marriage or your spouse. The issue is what anchors you and your marriage. Shelves can only handle the amount of weight that the anchors will support. Marriage can only handle the amount of weight that the anchor supports. So many of our Christian marriages point to communication, money, parenting, and intimacy as the problems that keep our marriage from thriving. But, the real problem in the marriage is that it isn't correctly anchored. So, it's just a matter of time before things come crashing down. Other well-intended Christians are praying for God to bless their marriage with the abundance that scripture promises. But, God won't do that because He knows your marriage would collapse under the weight of the responsibility because it isn't well anchored. The question then is what truly anchors Christian marriage and how deeply are those anchors grounded?

Prayer Lesson 4
Pray for a Christ-Anchored Marriage   **Hebrews 6:18-19**

Every time you choose to trust God's voice rather than your own, you drive that spiritual anchor deeper in your soul. Every time you choose to trust yourself, you loosen that spiritual anchor. If we couples truly trusted God more than ourselves, our homes would be shining examples of humility and grace. We would be paragons of generosity to those in spiritual and financial need. Our marriages would be exemplars that others wish to emulate. Instead, we step timidly from one situation to the next, hoping that everything doesn't get worse. It is not easy to displace trust in ourselves with trust in God. It takes good teaching. It takes consistent accountability. And, it takes practice to keep choosing the Spirit over the flesh.

Let's Talk

MONDAY
- Thinking as fully as possible about home, work, school, church, and community settings in which you operate, what responsibilities feel heaviest to you? Which responsibilities feel easiest?
- Can you recall a time recently when your spouse added another responsibility to your plate without consulting you first? How can you agree together to not add to each other's responsibilities without first discussing it?

TUESDAY
- How well is your marriage handling the weight of responsibilities that you and others have placed upon it?
- What is happening in your lives right now that is pulling you away from spending more time with the Lord?

WEDNESDAY
- What one thing (big or small) is happening in your marriage today that you know is lacking the level of righteousness to which God is calling it?
- What simple thing(s) can you each do to more securely anchor this concern in the Lord?

THURSDAY
- Discuss ways in which you have blamed a lack of communication or conflict resolution skills for difficulties in your marriage that are really a lack of conviction by one or both of you to follow God's instructions for your spiritual health.
- What would help redirect your focus to the spiritual core of your marriage when you are feeling frustrated with your spouse?

FRIDAY
- This week's lesson suggests that the best anchor is learning to trust God's voice more than you trust your own will. When and how do you best discern God's voice?
- What daily steps can you take as a couple to listen better for God's voice? If you can do this, how would this impact your marriage?

Prayer Lesson 4
Pray for a Christ-Anchored Marriage

Hebrews 6:18-19

Let's Reflect

> Pray for a Christ-Anchored Marriage

As you reflect on this week's lesson and questions, identify one behavior that the Holy Spirit is convicting each of you to change in order that your marriage has stronger anchors in the Lord. In the space below, record what behavior is going to be different going forward.

_____

_____

_____

_____

_____

_____

MONDAY

Dear Lord, forgive us for the times that we have not consulted you before adding more duties to our schedule. Teach us to better discern when to say 'yes' and when to say 'no' to adding more to our plates. Give us the wisdom to leave room in our lives and schedules to first say 'yes' to the things you desire of us. Help us to anchor our marriage in you so that it does not collapse. In the name of the Absolute Jesus Christ of Nazareth we pray. Amen.

TUESDAY

Dear Lord, we know that you promise in your word (1 Corinthians 10:13) to not to put more on us than we can bear. So, we know the weight we feel is an opportunity for us to slow down and seek your will for us. Change is hard. But, we are asking that you will strengthen our marriage so that we can better share responsibilities. We are asking for courage to release responsibilities from our lives that are pulling us away from our commitments to you and to one another. In the name of the Absolute Jesus Christ of Nazareth we pray. Amen.

WEDNESDAY

Dear Lord, there are areas in our marriage that are falling well short of the righteous standard that you give us in scripture. Thank you for the grace you've given us to bring these shortcomings in line with your Word. We want to be God-honoring in all that we say and do. Therefore, we commit ourselves to incremental improvement until you are pleased with us. In the name of the Absolute Jesus Christ of Nazareth we pray. Amen.

THURSDAY

Dear Lord, we are better at understanding how many of the cracks that we see and feel in our marriage have spiritual issues at the core. We know that the challenges and responsibilities of daily life are eroding our spirit and soul because we are not as anchored in you as we need to be. We want to stop repeating the same negative patterns over and over again. We pray for healing of our hearts and a renewed mind so that our first responses are gratitude and humility towards you and each other. Help us to feel the joy of the Lord as our strength. In the name of the Absolute Jesus Christ of Nazareth we pray. Amen.

FRIDAY

Dear Lord, we want and need to hear your voice more as we learn a more righteous way in our marriage. We know that most of our marital struggles are a result of acting in our own ego and pride without listening well to what you are saying to us through your Holy Spirit. We know your ways are far higher than ours and your thoughts are far higher than our thoughts. We want your will more than our own will to be done. Help our will to decrease so that you have the freedom to flow in our marriage as you will. In the name of the Absolute Jesus Christ of Nazareth we pray. Amen.

PRAY FOR DIVINE FAVOR

REFERENCE SCRIPTURE

"For the LORD God is a sun and shield; the LORD bestows favor and honor; no good thing does he withhold from those whose walk is blameless."
—Psalm 84:11, NIV.

BREATH PRAYER

May the favor of God lead us through all of our uncertainty.

OBJECT STORY
FENCES AND FAVOR

It all started when I (Harold) came home from the gym and was startled to see a dead deer in our driveway. I wondered what could have happened to this deer and what to do about it. Then, I noticed that a large section of the iron-wrought fence spanning the entire width along the front of our property had fallen to the ground. While I don't know exactly when the previous owners of this house erected the fence, it is pretty safe to assume the fence is probably as old as I am. We called the police, as we had initially assumed that a car must have hit this heavy fence in an unsuccessful effort to avoid the deer. But, when the police arrived, the officer explained, "We see it a lot. The deer tried to jump the fence and got impaled on one of the iron spikes and pulled the fence over as it tried to free itself." Gross.

My condolences to the deer...but what about my fence? One call to our home insurance company confirmed that we had coverage to replace the fence. Another call to a fence company secured an estimate. One final piece was needed: a permit from the township office.

Here's where the trouble started. The Assistant Deputy of Inspection's search through the historical records found no evidence that the original owners of this 80-year-old house were ever issued a permit to erect a fence. And, current ordinances allow fences only along the side and the rear of a property—absolutely not in the front. "Mr. Arnold, you are not allowed to replace your current fence with a new one."

I was flabbergasted. The Assistant Deputy saw the frustration in my face and eventually said, "wait here." As I stood there, a sudden impulse in my spirit said, Pray for favor. Pray for favor right now. I closed my eyes and bowed my head. "Lord, I don't know if this fence situation matters to you.

But, it is a pretty big deal for me. And, if you see fit to work this out on our behalf and have this township show us favor, I will do my best to make sure you get the glory for it. Thank you in advance. Amen." I opened my eyes and waited.

A few minutes later the Assistant Deputy of Inspections returned and told me that she went to the Chief Inspector to advocate for my case. The Chief Inspector said, "Just tell him no." She asked again. He repeated the same thing. She walked out of his office, feeling defeated. As she was walking back down the hall towards me, she said that she felt something in her spirit tell her to go back to the Chief Inspector once more. But, she hesitated because she wondered if she would be placing her own job in jeopardy. But, she decided to take the risk. In returning to the Chief Inspector's office she said, "This is not right. Mr. Arnold has done nothing wrong and this situation is out of his control. I will not go and tell him that he cannot rebuild his fence." In so many words, the Chief Inspector replied, "If you feel that strongly about it, go ahead and give him the permit."

As I listened to her recount this minor miracle, all I could do was thank the Lord. I told her that I had felt a sudden urge to pray for favor. She said, "Amen. Well, your prayers were answered."

Why are we recounting this story of a fence permit to you? The Lord settled in our spirit that day that this is a season of favor for those who are chasing after Him.

And, we encourage Christ followers in this season to ardently pursue God now and pray for favor. The Adversary will definitely create chaos and doubt as you pursue. Even so, desire His divine will (over your own willfulness) and expect divine favor as you do so.

We know that you may have much bigger needs than a fence permit. And, we know it can feel risky to be so vulnerable in your expectation of God to meet that need. But, the Lord is waiting for you both to truly desire that work so that he can relentlessly pour his favor upon your life and your marriage.

Let's Talk

MONDAY
- What does it mean to you to have God's favor in your marriage? In what ways do you feel God's favor in your marriage?
- When, if ever, has your marriage been out of God's favor?

TUESDAY
- God often uses other people as an act of His favor. Who have been agents of God's divine favor in your marriage?
- How have you expressed your gratitude to the Lord when His favor is evident in your marriage? Are there times you have taken God's favor for granted?

WEDNESDAY
- Why do you believe God has specifically chosen your marriage as a recipient of His favor?
- What responsibility comes with God's favor?

THURSDAY
- God's favor is most evident when you follow the Spirit in taking risks for the Kingdom. What risks are the Holy Spirit inviting you to take as a couple so that God can be glorified?
- Despite your good intentions, what fears and worries make it difficult for you to take risks together?

FRIDAY
- It is God's intention for you to be agents of God's transforming favor for other believers. Who do you think this might be? Brainstorm and pray about how the Lord is preparing them and you.
- Pray about what the Lord needs to do in you as a couple to position you as agents of favor for others.

Prayer Lesson 5
Pray for Divine Favor

Psalm 84:11

Let's Reflect

Pray for Divine Favor

This week your reflections and prayers are favor focused. In your Christian walk, there is nothing finer than God's favor. Without God's favor, we cannot experience life more abundantly (John 10:10). Without God's favor, we cannot be more than conquerors (Romans 8:37). Record the ways God's favor has been evident in the abundance and conquering you have witnessed as each of you has begun to invest more in your marriage.

_____

_____

_____

_____

_____

_____

Let's Pray

MONDAY

Dear Lord, in your presence there is forgiveness and divine favor. You always love us. But, your favor means that you privilege us—like you did David over the other sons of Jesse. You select us to be blessed like you did for Abraham and Sarah. You elevate us as the bedrock of your Church like you did for the Apostle Peter. Your favor in our marriage is undeserved. It is another of your many acts of grace towards us. Yet, we know that you favor those who are faithful to you. We ask that your Holy Spirit continue to guide us towards the faithfulness so that we are never outside your favor. In the name of the Absolute Jesus Christ of Nazareth we pray. Amen.

TUESDAY

Dear Lord, we are grateful for the unexpected ways you have shown your favor in our marriage. Sometimes, your favor comes through unexpected people. At other times, your favor flows from unexpected places and circumstances. We never want to be the kind of couple that takes your favor for granted as your children often have. We want to both remember and to proclaim to all of those in our circle of influence how you made a way when there was no way. Scripture records several instances when people excitedly ran and told of your miracle in their life. Our prayer today is that we will be vessels of honor that are just as excited to proclaim your goodness and favor to a distracted and lost world. In the name of the Absolute Jesus Christ of Nazareth we pray. Amen.

WEDNESDAY

Dear Lord, your Holy Word is full of miracles in both the Old and New Testaments. In the Old Testament, your faithful prophets like Elijah and Jeremiah acted on your behalf to perform supernatural acts. In the New Testament, just a touch or a word from Jesus was enough to transform a life from broken to whole. Our prayer is that we will mature into a spiritual team to do your righteous work. Our prayer is that your touch can heal our areas of spiritual blindness like the physical blindness of Bartimaeus (Mark 10:46). As a couple, we offer ourselves as faithful agents of your divine favor. In the name of the Absolute Jesus Christ of Nazareth we pray. Amen.

THURSDAY

Dear Lord, we know that you are the Way, the Truth, and the Life. As the Way, we know that your ways are higher than our ways. As the Truth, we know that carrying our cross like Christ is the only path to salvation. As the Life, we know that everything outside of you leads to death. We know these things in our heads. Yet, our hearts still yearn to forge our own way, define our own truth, and control our own lives. We have been afraid to take the risks necessary to worship you in spirit and in truth. But, as a couple, we will find your favor again. In the name of the Absolute Jesus Christ of Nazareth we pray. Amen.

FRIDAY

Dear Lord, one thing that we've learned is that favor isn't fair—meaning it isn't distributed equally to everyone. Favor cannot be scripted according to our human will or behaviors. But, what we have learned is that favor closely follows you—likes ripples in the wake of your Spirit in motion. Though we have fallen out of the shadow of your favor at times, we are determined to do the work to experience the fullness of your favor and to share that with others. In the name of the Absolute Jesus Christ of Nazareth we pray. Amen.

PRAY FOR A SPIRIT-FILLED MARITAL AGENDA

REFERENCE SCRIPTURE

"He said to him a second time, 'Simon, son of John, do you love me?' He said to him, 'Yes, Lord; you know that I love you.' He said to him, 'Tend my sheep."—John 21:16, ESV.

BREATH PRAYER

Order our steps such that when we arrive at each destination there is no doubt in our minds that your perfect will brought us there.

OBJECT STORY
IT'S TIME TO CLEAN HOUSE

Shortly after New Year's, we always find it fascinating to watch the gym swell with people. They are everywhere—huffing and puffing and sweating. But, most of them will be gone by March. We see the pattern every year. They made a New Year's resolution to exercise more or to lose weight. They get through January and maybe February. But, the visits become spaced farther and farther apart as the weeks go by. Eventually, they stop coming altogether. They have great intentions, but fail to adopt the gym as a long-term solution. By the end of the first quarter, all will be back to normal at the gym. The long-term gym members have figured out that exercise and regular visits to the gym is part of their solution to fitness or health-related concerns. They keep coming to the gym because they have benefitted from the results.

Resolution only starts the action. It takes discipline and consistency to shift from resolution to solution in accomplishing much of anything in life. Your focus must switch from resolution to do "something" to understanding what that "something" solves for you.

We met with a group of couples in our local marriage ministry and challenged them to set an annual agenda for their marriage. Yes, an agenda. The reality is that most of us don't think about an agenda for marriage. We see the purpose of an agenda at our jobs or maybe in our church meetings. We like agendas in these settings because they help everyone understand the objectives of the meeting. Agendas help the meeting stay on track in order to accomplish the stated objective.

But, why are we skeptical of an agenda for our marriage? Isn't it important for spouses to understand the objectives of their marriage? Isn't it vital to know if you're staying on track to accomplishing those objectives? So, why do we not think about an agenda in the marriage context? Well, somehow it feels out of place, doesn't it? It feels too constricting and controlling. It seems to take away our flexibility. Not true.

Many Christian couples want to have a great marriage. They want to feel happy and secure. So, these well-meaning couples set out a resolution for the new year. They might, for example, commit to have a date night every month this year. It is their resolution. You know what happens though, don't you? The job demands get too hectic or the kids' schedules take over. After a few attempts, the date night resolution is over. But, what if this same couple focused on the problem in need of a solution? What if they admitted that they lacked intimacy, feared drifting apart, or wanted to set an example for their children as they cultivated their relationship? If they focus on the "why" of the resolution, then they would be much more likely to follow through on the solution—the monthly date night. This is the fundamental reason why an agenda is so important for your marriage. You and your spouse will benefit from a shared "why" as well as agreement on the solutions to achieve it. Setting an agenda for your marriage this year is a bold step to getting there.

So, we hope this week that you both will sit down, reflect, and pray about each element of your agenda. We guarantee that it will change the dynamic of your relationship. And, yes, your commitment to praying through this book that you have in your hands is a great place to anchor your agenda.

Prayer Lesson 6
Pray for a Spirit-filled Marital Agenda

John 21:16

Let's Talk

MONDAY
- What goals have you set for this year as a couple? Are these goals from God?
- How successful have you been over the years in reaching the annual goals that you set?

TUESDAY
- How important is it to each of you that you reach your marital goals? Why?
- What are the implications of not reaching your goals?

WEDNESDAY
- What do you see as the benefits and limitations of setting an agenda to help you reach your marital goals?
- At a high level, what might an agenda for this year look like for your marriage?

THURSDAY
- How have you reacted in the past when God interrupts your agenda for your marriage with an agenda of His own that doesn't accommodate your agenda?
- What is your process for developing shared goals as a couple when you initially have vastly different perspectives as to what the agenda should entail to reach those goals?

FRIDAY
- Is it more important for you to develop and reach individual goals each of you may have or a shared goal for your marriage? What evidence supports your answer?
- How resolved are you to glorify God with your marital goals?

John 21:16

Prayer Lesson 6
Pray for a Spirit-filled Marital Agenda

Let's Reflect

> Pray for a Spirit-filled Marital Agenda

This week your reflections and prayers focus on goals, especially on contrasting self-directed goals versus God-directed goals. Sometimes the difference is clear. But, at other times it is difficult to reliably tease them apart. Take a sheet of paper and identify your 1-year and 3-year goals as a couple. Place an asterisk beside each goal which you both agree is from God without a shadow of doubt. Share with each other what gives you such confidence that God is directing that goal.

_____

_____

_____

_____

_____

_____

Let's Pray

MONDAY

Dear Lord, your Word tells us that our plans will always succeed if our resolve is to commit to you whatever we do (Proverbs 16:3). Our commitment to our plans is sometimes firm and fervent and at other times it is lax. Part of our wavering commitment is a lack of confidence that our plans will succeed. If we knew they were guaranteed to succeed it would probably be much easier for us to stay consistent with executing our agenda. When we remain centered in you, our plans must succeed, because they aren't actually our plans. They are your plans. May we have the conviction to follow you such that your goals are reflected in the way that we do marriage. Help us to make the daily choices that take us one step closer to bringing your Kingdom to the world in which we live. In the name of the Absolute Jesus Christ of Nazareth we pray. Amen.

TUESDAY

Dear Lord, we would not be honest if we said it wasn't important to us to achieve the goals that we've set. Achieving our goals helps us to feel like we are moving forward in our life and not just treading water. But the trouble with our goal setting is that often it doesn't reflect both of our desires because it can be hard to find a place of agreement. Other times, our busy schedules make it hard for us to allocate the necessary time to hash out a plan. But, our bigger problem is that we typically neglect coming to you with ideas and an open mind and sufficient time such that we can allow your Holy Spirit to lead our planning process. More often than not, we want to tell you our plan and just ask you to bless it. Will you give us the wisdom to seek your will first? In the name of the Absolute Jesus Christ of Nazareth we pray. Amen.

WEDNESDAY

Dear Lord, how do we as a couple become a channel for you on this earth? We are reminded of the rich young ruler in scripture who asked you about eternal life (Mark 10:16-31). You told him to sell all that he had and to follow you. We have to ask ourselves if we have really sold ourselves out so that we could go where you lead us. As the rich young ruler's failure demonstrates, it is hard to leave everything behind. He was attracted to Jesus and sought the key to eternal life. But, he wanted the material things of this world even more. Forgive us as a couple for all the ways in which we seek pleasures of the flesh more than abiding in the center of your will. Only through your grace and the power of the Holy Spirit can we be sold out for whatever you have in store for us. In the name of the Absolute Jesus Christ of Nazareth we pray. Amen.

THURSDAY

Dear Lord, we have felt utterly defeated when seemingly solid dreams and plans seemed to fall apart all around us—often for reasons that felt totally out of our control. It's easy to become discouraged when things just don't go our way or we encounter one obstacle after another. The only thing that keeps us going sometimes is our faith that your plans for us are greater than anything that we could come up with on our own. So, even in our discouragement, we strive to trust the process that you are taking us through. We long to be in the company of other couples that are also stretching themselves beyond what feels like failure. We declare with assuredness that everything that you have for us will reach us, as long as we are grounded in you. We ask you to interrupt any plans of the Adversary that seek to hinder your blessing from us. In the name of the Absolute Jesus Christ of Nazareth we pray. Amen.

FRIDAY

Dear Lord, we are proud of the many things that we have been able to achieve as a couple. Some of them are big things that required a lot of attention, time, and sacrifice. Others are small things that felt like a big win for us. We cannot thank you enough for the role of the Holy Spirit in helping us balance each other's needs in a way that left each of us feeling affirmed. But, even with our accomplishments, we want you to see us as trusted children who will use our marriage to care for your sheep (John 21:16). Just like you informed the Apostle Peter that if he loved you to feed your sheep, give us the wisdom, the resources, and the courage to love and serve those in our path of influence. If that requires us to change direction, endow us with the divine anointing to change tactics with joy so that you may be glorified. Encourage us to have a profound sense of gratitude for all of the privileges that surround us. Keep us humble so that we hold our accomplishments lightly and are ready to let go when you tell us. This is our earnest desire even in our imperfections. In the name of the Absolute Jesus Christ of Nazareth we pray. Amen.

PRAY FOR CONFIDENCE IN GOD'S PROMISES

REFERENCE SCRIPTURE

"Count it all joy, my brothers, when you meet trials of various kinds, for you know that the testing of your faith produces steadfastness. And let steadfastness have its full effect, that you may be perfect and complete, lacking in nothing."—James 1:2-4, ESV.

BREATH PRAYER

Fill our minds with an overwhelming sense of peace that demonstrates your constant presence with us as a couple.

OBJECT STORY

PROTECTING YOUR MIND AND MARRIAGE FROM THE THIEF

We excitedly boarded the train in Trenton, NJ for the hour and a half ride to Newark International Airport, where we would catch our flight for our much-anticipated vacation. I (Harold) was so excited for two blissful weeks of mental peace. But, within ten minutes, it was gone. Stolen.

We were only minutes into the train ride when out of nowhere my mind told me that I forgot to lock the car. I had dropped Dalia off at the train station with our luggage and then proceeded down the block to park the car. I found a suitable parking spot and then I remembered jumping out of the car, grabbing my backpack, and heading to the train station. But, did I lock the car? As we sat on the north-bound train moving farther and farther away from our car, I kept trying to visualize whether I pressed the lock on the remote. I couldn't remember doing so. The more I thought about it, the more I became convinced that I didn't lock our practically new car. My mind swirled. The car is going to be stolen or vandalized! I can't get off the train to check, or we'll miss our flight...how could I be so dumb? All I had to do was push the stupid lock button!

I feared telling Dalia that I don't think I locked the car because I didn't want her worrying about it too. Our vacation was supposed to be about mental peace, yet I was tormented. I couldn't let go of the thought that my vacation was ruined before it even got started. It finally occurred to me that in all this negative rumination, I had completely lost any sense of God's presence. The words of the prophet Isaiah (26:3) came to my mind: "You keep him in perfect peace whose mind is stayed on you, because he trusts in you." I needed peace. So, I prayed. I begged the Lord to give me peace and rest in Him for the next two weeks regardless of what might happen to our car. I prayed that I could forgive myself—even if the worst happened to the car.

As I sat in prayer and meditation that day, the Lord gave me a powerful vision of an angel brandishing a sword radiant with light and standing guard right beside our red Toyota Camry. Then, I felt the words in my Spirit, I'm standing guard. Do not worry any longer. When I arose from that prayer, my spirit was settled. Over the next two weeks, my mind rarely even thought about the car.

The Adversary seeks to steal your joy by stoking fears of the worst possible outcomes. He steals your contentment by focusing your attention on all of the things you don't have. He steals your peace by stoking your worries. He steals your marriage by reminding you of the shortcomings of your spouse. He steals your generosity and replaces it with a scarcity mindset. Ultimately, and most perniciously, he steals your faith by keeping you focused on the present rather than the promise. The Apostle John captured it best, "The thief comes only to steal and kill and destroy" (John 10:10). The Adversary plays mind games to destroy what God has for your life, marriage, and family. He is lying to you.

We are writing this to remind you of a single Truth that the Apostle Paul posits, "And I am sure of this, that he who began a good work in you will bring it to completion at the day of Jesus Christ" (Philippians 1:6). Whatever God has started, He will finish as long as you keep trusting and delighting in Him. Trust Him with your marriage. Trust Him with your children.

Trust Him with your money. Trust Him with your health. Surrender your mind to Christ and ask Him for peace, especially in the midst of a difficult storm. We're believing right now that Christ and His assigned heavenly angels are standing guard over his promises to you with a flaming sword. The Adversary is lying to you in order to steal what God has promised you. But, the Truth is that God is working things out for your glorious end (Jeremiah 29:11), "For I know the plans I have for you" declares the Lord, "plans to prosper you and not to harm you, plans to give you hope and a future." Dalia and I arrived back from vacation two

Prayer Lesson 7
Pray for Confidence in God's Promises — James 1:2-4

weeks later. There sitting in the garage was our car—the doors were locked all along!

Let's talk

MONDAY
- In your marriage, what are some examples of when and how the Adversary disrupts your peace of mind?
- What negative thoughts do you tend to rehearse in your mind? Confess those to God and one another. And pray for one another so you may be healed (James 5:16)

TUESDAY
- What has the enemy of the Lord stolen from your marriage? For how long have you felt this way?
- How has this missing element impacted your marriage?

WEDNESDAY
- In your marriage, which of you is more of a worrier? How does worry keep your marriage from being its best?
- How does the worrier's mindset make it more difficult to trust in God? How can the spouse that worries less be of assistance to the spouse that worries more?

THURSDAY
- In your marriage, when do you most feel God's presence? Give a couple of examples.
- As a Christian couple, how could you practically help each other to enter God's presence when one or both of you is feeling anxious and worried?

FRIDAY
- What are some examples of times that God has shown up, even though you doubted Him, and proven to you that you can trust Him to bless your marriage?
- Name at least one thing that is happening in your marriage right now that God wants you to surrender to Him so He can work it out for His glory. Will you give it to Him?

Prayer Lesson 7
Pray for Confidence in God's Promises

James 1:2-4

Let's Reflect

> Pray for Confidence in God's Promises

As you reflect on this week's lesson and questions, recount what the Enemy has stolen from you as a couple and what you are committed to do to take back what belongs to you. In the space below, record who the Lord is inviting you to become and what He is encouraging you to do.

_____

_____

_____

_____

_____

_____

MONDAY

Dear Lord, you tell us in your Word that you will keep us in perfect peace as we keep our minds stayed on you. But, we often struggle to maintain a peaceful attitude, given some of the things that happen in our home and marriage. Sometimes, it feels impossible to maintain peacefulness. Peace is a fruit of the Spirit of God and we ask you to help us to welcome peace and banish negative thoughts, fear and anxiety. We know from the Beatitudes that peacemakers are blessed. We need your Holy Spirit to transform us into a couple who is blessed by the peace that only comes from above. In the name of the Absolute Jesus Christ of Nazareth we pray. Amen.

TUESDAY

Dear Lord, you declared that the Adversary is a thief who comes to steal, kill, and destroy all of the goodness in our lives and marriage. Like Adam and Eve, we have listened too often to the lies and fears that Satan tells us. We know now that he mostly just wants to steal our joy and your glory. We ask your forgiveness for doubting you and listening to him. We want back everything that the Enemy has stolen. And, we know that it begins with surrendering our past brokenness and selfish ambitions to you. We put these on your altar today. In the name of the Absolute Jesus Christ of Nazareth we pray. Amen.

WEDNESDAY

Dear Lord, our marriage is suffocating with worry—sometimes small things and other time big worries. Help us to see the futility of worrying about things that are behind us and about things that are in the future. The past is over. And, only you know the future. Help us to trust that you are redeeming the mistakes of our past and orchestrating the steps towards our future as we learn to trust more in you. We know that sometimes bad things happen to good people. But, we want to trust that you will never put more on us than we can handle when we walk according to the Spirit. In the name of the Absolute Jesus Christ of Nazareth we pray. Amen.

THURSDAY

Dear Lord, your presence brings peace, joy, gentleness, long-suffering, and all the other fruit of the Spirit. But, many times as a couple we fail to create an atmosphere where your Spirit is welcome to do its work. Our self-righteous bickering creates tension and division in our home. Your Word tells us that a house that is divided cannot stand. We want to stand and endure. Will you help us to create an atmosphere in our marriage where the Light of Christ exposes our dark tendencies and allows you to be fully present? In the name of the Absolute Jesus Christ of Nazareth we pray. Amen.

FRIDAY

Dear Lord, we are tired of the Adversary taking from us the fruit and harvest that you have for us. We are tired of eating crumbs where you intend for us to feast. We are tired of thinking about what we lack when we know that you are a God of plenty. We have not centered our hearts and minds on you. But, that's changing now. As the Apostle Paul encourages us, renew our minds and strengthen the work of the Holy Spirit within us. We want to live day-by-day in your presence, whatever the cost, because we understand the reward. In the name of the Absolute Jesus Christ of Nazareth we pray. Amen.

PRAY FOR GODLY DISCIPLINE

REFERENCE SCRIPTURE

"Have nothing to do with irreverent, silly myths. Rather train yourself for godliness; for while bodily training is of some value, godliness is of value in every way, as it holds promise for the present life and also for the life to come."—1 Timothy 4:7-8, ESV.

BREATH PRAYER

Thank you for the suffering of Christ which gives us the grace to discipline our flesh.

OBJECT STORY

LIVING A GOLD MEDAL MARRIAGE

We absolutely love the Olympics. There is something about watching the athletes who are the absolute best in the world compete at the highest level. How do these athletes prepare for these opportunities on the world's largest stage that happens only once every four years? Yes, most are amazingly gifted physically. But these Olympians demonstrate extraordinary discipline in training their body and their mind for peak performance. While we can admire the athletic feats of these Olympic marvels, it behooves us to remember that God calls us to do more extraordinary feats than these Olympians—and more often than every four years. And, the eternal stakes are even higher when it comes to the synchronized maturity needed for peak performance in marriage.

Here are a few examples of the disciplines "Coach Jesus" trains us to perform as married couples:

- **Submit your marriage as a tithe:** As the Lord blesses your marriage, give from this bounty to together bless and encourage others. It takes discipline to tithe your marriage, especially when you are disappointed with it.
- **Serve your spouse's needs first:** Listen to discern your spouse's deepest need and consider ways you can prioritize this need. It takes discipline to serve this graciously because it demands humility.
- **Sacrifice anything that hinders your spiritual witness as a couple:** Your marriage is designed to be a testimony of God's miracle of knitting two sinful beings into one sanctified relationship. It takes discipline to witness this sacrificially.

Prayer Lesson 8
Pray for Godly Discipline   1 Timothy 4:7-8

The amazing thing about Coach Jesus is that the discipline He demands of us is easy and light (Matthew 11:28-30). Coach Jesus instructs us to prayerfully practice these steps today and then do it again tomorrow and the next day. If you choose your own training path, you will feel the burden of the load. Your (training) ways that seem right to you are leading to the destruction of your marriage (Proverbs 14:12). Your soul (and your marriage) is longing for the Divine Coach. It takes a measure of grace to remain disciplined through the ebbs and flows of Christian marriage. The Apostle Paul tells his disciple Timothy that he must "train himself for godliness" (1 Timothy 4:7). This admonition, however, is just as relevant for us today. Godliness is gold (and the goal).

My favorite story from the 2022 Summer Olympics was the journey of U.S. sprinter Allyson Felix. During these games, Felix became the most decorated U.S. track and field Olympian of all time. After her record-setting Olympics, Felix said, "Everyone sees the glory moments, but they don't see what happens behind the scenes." My prayer is that you and I can both train with Coach Jesus through His proven training program so that we too can embody the graceful small steps necessary to claim the gold of godliness in our marriages.

Let's Talk

MONDAY
- Given the amount of investment that you make into your marriage, would you describe your marriage as amateur or professional?
- What similarities do you see between what it takes to excel in athletics versus marriage?

TUESDAY
- One encouragement from this week's lesson is to tithe your marriage. What does it mean to you to give the first fruit of your marriage as a tithe?
- How do you compare tithing of your income with tithing of your marriage?

WEDNESDAY
- Humility is the greatest key to growth in marriage. As a couple, how do you share humility with each other? When is humility difficult?
- In what way do you most desire your spouse to serve you?

THURSDAY
- What is one personality flaw that each of you have that compromises your marriage's witness for Christ and the Kingdom of God?
- How have these personality characteristics put distance between you as a couple?

FRIDAY
- What is one small adjustment that each of you can make in your marriage that could make a huge impact in your relationship?
- If this small adjustment was made, what impact do you believe that would have?

Prayer Lesson 8
Pray for Godly Discipline

1 Timothy 4:7-8

Let's Reflect

> Pray for Godly Discipline

This week your reflections and prayers are on the spiritual and relational preparation and training involved in building a gold medal marriage. Summarize here a one-week schedule of the specific actions you can take as a couple to train your marriage for godliness. Once you've laid out the schedule, commit yourselves to implementing it next week.

_____

_____

_____

_____

_____

_____

_____

Let's Pray

MONDAY

Dear Lord, all that is good comes from you. You are the air we breathe and the spring in our step. All that is worthy, honorable, and true is found in you. We want to walk worthy of you in our relationship together. We want our marriage to be an accurate reflection of your largesse. As the Apostle Paul encourages, we want to press towards the mark for the prize of the high calling in Christ Jesus. Your high calling is not only our prize but is our honor. We repent to you for the many times when we have not pressed for your highest calling for our marriage. We know that we must train ourselves to build up these muscles in our marriage. We cannot do it without you. In the name of the Absolute Jesus Christ of Nazareth we pray. Amen.

TUESDAY

Dear Lord, your Word teaches us the principle of tithing as a practice of honoring you with the best of our harvest. We know our entire harvest belongs to you but you permit us to choose how ninety percent is spent. Similarly, our entire marriage belongs to you but you permit us to choose how much we offer our marriage as an acceptable offering to you. We may have never thought about the need to tithe our marriage before. But, we see how it is a symbol of our trust in you to bless our union commensurate with the measure that we give our marriage to you. Your Word tells us that the same measure we give is the measure that we receive. So, Lord expand the measure that our marriage gives so that you can expand our capacity to receive from you. In the name of the Absolute Jesus Christ of Nazareth we pray. Amen.

Prayer Lesson 8
Pray for Godly Discipline　　　　　　　　　　　　　　1 Timothy 4:7-8

WEDNESDAY

Dear Lord, relationship with you requires humility for us as a couple. For us, that can be hard. And, because it is hard, sometimes we just don't do it very well. But, you modeled sacrifice and humility in giving your Son to die for us. There is no greater love that could be shown that Jesus' blood shed for us as individuals and as a couple in covenant with you. Jesus died so that we can die to our own selfishness. Jesus died so that we can be redeemed and redeem one another through the grace of your Holy Spirit. We are sorry for our lapses in pride. Forgive our hubris and ego. It really is only through your mercy that humility in our marriage is possible. In the name of the Absolute Jesus Christ of Nazareth we pray. Amen.

THURSDAY

Dear Lord, we know that you tell us in the Holy Scripture that each of us is fearfully and wonderfully made. You know the intimate details of our lives and you love us still. Yet, we know that aspects of our personality, thoughts, and desires do not align with your Word and your will. Our personalities often rub each other the wrong way and feel like sand in our shoes. It can be irritating. Even in the difficulty of differing and sometimes conflicting personality traits, we sense in our spirit that this is part of your process for forming us into the image of Christ. Help us to surrender what feels familiar when it stands in the way of our effective witness for you. In the name of the Absolute Jesus Christ of Nazareth we pray. Amen.

FRIDAY

Dear Lord, help us to do the many small tasks behind the scenes of our marriage so that we build our trust in you and one another. Help us to avoid the hypocrisy of perpetrating a relationship that we don't really have. Help us to accept the value of marginal gains that steadily bring our hearts in alignment with yours. Help us to see when we are veering off track in the way we treat each other. Help us to hold onto our own desires lightly in deference to your desires for us. We know we are nothing without you. Our hopes and future are with you. Our best way forward is only through you because you are the Way, the Truth, and the Life. In the name of the Absolute Jesus Christ of Nazareth we pray. Amen.

PRAY FOR PRESENCE TOGETHER

REFERENCE SCRIPTURE

"Do two walk together, unless they have agreed to meet?"
—Amos 3:3, NIV.

BREATH PRAYER

Dear Lord, may your divine presence draw us into being fully present in our marriage.

OBJECT STORY

WHERE DO LOST SOCKS GO?

In general, when I (Harold) make up my mind to take care of the laundry, I do a good job of getting the clothes sorted into hot, warm, and cold piles and getting them through the washer and dryer gauntlet. After removing them from the dryer, I toss them into the laundry basket and, well…I lose my motivation. I just don't like folding the clothes and putting them away. But, what I really (seriously really) hate are the socks. I think I could face the rest of it if I didn't have to deal with those annoying socks.

Inevitably, just when I'm a few socks away from finishing my toil, I'm stuck. Where is the matching sock for this one? Where is the match for that one? I washed all of the clothes in the hamper. I'm sure neither Dalia nor I just wore one sock. Where in the world is the other sock? So, in my exasperation, I leave all the single socks in the basket. The same thing happens to Dalia. We figure eventually the other one will show up. As the weeks and months pass, one laundry load after another, the number of unmatched socks grows. But, where do lost socks go? I'm sure the six-year-old versions of us would just blame the sock gremlins. But really, where do lost socks go?

Though somewhat facetious, it is relevant because, without its match, the sock is useless. And, herein lies one of the most important lessons that we've learned about marriage: Without my mate, my marriage is useless. Don't get me wrong. It doesn't mean that either of us are useless. God created us each with innate and inherent value. But, my marriage is useless for the purposes for which God ordained it.

Prayer Lesson 9
Pray for Presence Together

Amos 3:3

God intended for us to be equal in every way. On that much anticipated summer day, more than thirty-five years ago, we vowed to become a mutually submissive pair. But, it has taken us decades to learn and embody what that really means. In the early days, Dalia sometimes struggled with loneliness while Harold pecked away on his computer keyboard in the other room. If she became frustrated with him for any reason, Harold rationalized away her response and chalked it up as her being too emotional. If things that she prioritized weren't that important to Harold, he often ignored them. She didn't feel that Harold listened to her. Harold admits being too immature to understand the difference between hearing and listening.

For her part, Dalia also realized that Harold sometimes struggled with loneliness because she would not keep up with the ideas that crowded his brain or stayed up late nights with him as she sensed he would sometimes desire. Dalia describes not wanting to sacrifice her time for rest and relaxation to be there for Harold.

Don't get us wrong. We had some good aspects to our marriage as well. But, the essence of us as a pair—the potential for what God wanted to do in and with us as a couple—was missing. And, for many years, we didn't even know the magnitude of the problem.

We are not alone in this struggle. As counselors and marriage ministry leaders, we have heard countless laments from the Christian wife who feels alone in marriage—suffering loneliness and often mental health challenges as she goes through her routines of home, work, and even ministry without the emotional (and often physical) presence of her husband. We've witnessed numerous accounts of the Christian husband who is alone in marriage—disoriented in his priorities, distanced from his children, and over invested in work and sports because he struggles to find the balance that his wife would bring to his life.

On and on it goes with seemingly no end in sight. Here we are, a room full of lost socks touting how many years we have been married, when in fact we've been missing far longer than present. Staying in the same house, eating from the same fridge, and sleeping in the same bed without truly experiencing marriage as a pair.

Our only hope to re-unite the pair that stood face to face at the altar is to submit to the Holy Spirit to pair us through grace, sacrifice, and servanthood. Our lives and marriages must become evidence of God's presence. Through our own journey of spiritual formation over the past three years (daily morning devotionals alone, evening devotionals together, weekly fasting), Team Arnold has grown to finally get a better understanding of the power God intended for this pairing more than three decades ago. Dalia is excited about our marriage because she believes her husband is really hearing from God. Harold is excited about his marriage because finally we are both fully present—making us available for God's purposes.

So, really, where do lost socks go? We are still not sure. But, we do know that lost husbands and wives need to air out our dirty laundry and be convicted when we are "married but missing." Then, we must make the daily decision to pick up our cross and walk as a pair led by the Holy Spirit.

Prayer Lesson 9
Pray for Presence Together

Amos 3:3

Let's Talk

MONDAY
- What type of presence does your spouse most need from you?
- What are some of the things that distract you from being fully present when your spouse needs you most?

TUESDAY
- When do you feel alone in your marriage?
- What does alone feel like for you?

WEDNESDAY
- Since your wedding, how long did it take for you both to start thinking and acting like a pair rather than mostly solo thinking? Are you there yet?
- When you are acting in harmony as a couple, what type of things are happening?

THURSDAY
- When you allowed key aspects of your lives to go down separate tracks, what has that experience cost you spiritually and psychologically as a couple?
- How misaligned or aligned are your values, motivations, and goals as a couple?

FRIDAY
- What is the Holy Spirit showing you as a path to greater presence as a couple?
- In what ways do you expect your greater presence together to expand the presence of God's activity in your lives?

Let's Reflect

> Pray for Presence Together

This week your reflections and prayers focus on inviting the presence of God into your marriage such that it enables your physical and emotional presence with each other. Identify one area that you desire to be more consistent in being present with one another in the presence of God. Write about what it would mean to find that consistency.

_____

_____

_____

_____

_____

_____

Let's Pray

MONDAY

Dear Lord, in your Word you promise us that in your presence there is fulness of joy (Psalm 16:11). How do we better invite your presence into the daily routine of our marriage? Joy often feels lost in the hectic way that we do marriage. We need joy in the way we communicate. Our parenting needs more joy. We need joy when we look at our finances. We need joy in our physical intimacy. We need joy in planning for our future. Our prayer is that rekindling of joy will make us yearn more to be present with each other rather than the parallel lives we tend to lead. We want to make you the center of our joy so that as we worship you together, we are drawn to each other. In the name of the Absolute Jesus Christ of Nazareth we pray. Amen.

TUESDAY

Dear Lord, you designed us as social creatures. You anointed marriage to be the greatest human social relationship. As husband and wife, our companionship is supposed to point our hearts and minds back to you. But, what about when our selfish tendencies break the social covenant that marriage is intended to be? The more we experience these transgressions in our marriage, the more loneliness sets in. We start to think and act individually rather than as a team of two. This, of course, then just reinforces the loneliness even more. We've seen this pattern repeat itself time and again. We need the conviction of the Holy Spirit and the power to check our egos so that we can listen to your voice rather than that of the Adversary. Will you heal our egos so that our lonely hearts can heal? In the name of the Absolute Jesus Christ of Nazareth we pray. Amen.

WEDNESDAY

Dear Lord, before we even knew each other, you already knew how our different personalities would shape each of us into a couple of success and significance. Before we even were engaged or even dated, you had a plan for how the Holy Spirit would operate in such a way that our hearts and the hearts of others would be moved towards righteousness. You not only saw all of this before we married but before we were even born. That is humbling to think about. We ask your forgiveness for all the ways that we have disrupted your divine plan. You saw our potential but in your omniscience, you also saw the ways our individual struggles with sin would interrupt your intention for us. But, we want to walk in the wonder of your design for our marriage. With your grace and mercy, we will be the couple that demonstrates your Kingdom here on earth. In the name of the Absolute Jesus Christ of Nazareth we pray. Amen.

THURSDAY

Dear Lord, before we married, we thought agreement would be easy. It sure felt natural when we were dating. But, we struggle a lot with agreement. It seems every time we take one step forward we then end up taking two steps back. We just seem to be going around in circles over the same issues without any real resolution. We inevitably end up back at the same place—sometimes even worse because yet another fight ensued. The greater work that you have for us to do requires us to be a more emotionally healthy couple. The greater work requires that we develop more humility, gracefulness, and generosity. We don't have to be a finished product to do good things for you. But, we have to renounce the areas of sin in the way that we do marriage. We want to embrace a level of righteousness that unites us as the Holy Spirit within each of us draws us towards solidarity in Christ. In the name of the Absolute Jesus Christ of Nazareth we pray. Amen.

Prayer Lesson 9
Pray for Presence Together   Amos 3:3

FRIDAY

Dear Lord, thank you for the gift of each other. We are so grateful for who you gave us as a spouse. Just the fact that we both call you Lord is a gift. Your Holy Spirit continues to convict us to become the great individuals and a great couple that manifests you in the home, church, and workplace. We are so much more together than we could be alone. Help us to keep this truth at the front of our minds so that we never again take each other for granted. Show us our spouse the way that you see us. Remove the scales of sin from our eyes so that we are drawn to the beauty that our spouse manifests. Continue to do your redemptive work in each of us so that we each manifest the beauty that resides within us. Our prayer is that the beauty in each of us intertwines into a miraculous power to help, hold, and heal all of those in need of a touch from you. In the name of the Absolute Jesus Christ of Nazareth we pray. Amen.

PRAY FOR ABUNDANCE THROUGH ALIGNMENT

REFERENCE SCRIPTURE

"The time will come,' says the Lord, 'when the grain and grapes will grow faster than they can be harvested."—Amos 9:13, NLT.

BREATH PRAYER

Bless how we see our differences, such that they are believed to be critical to our own sanctification and those who witness our journey.

OBJECT STORY

THE BIKER'S GUIDE TO MARITAL ABUNDANCE

When we first married over thirty-five years ago, we purchased a matching pair of red and white Schwinn ten-speed bicycles. Though as a newly married twenty-something-year-old couple, we certainly didn't appreciate biking's full potential for us as a couple, it could have been the perfect metaphor for Christian marriage—a blissful couple casually traveling life together in the same direction at the same pace. But, our marriage was anything but a smooth leisurely ride. In fact, biking exposed definitive flaws in our marriage. One day Dalia shared with Harold her experience of their bike rides 'together.'

"I can't keep up with you," she reprimanded. "You speed ahead and leave me behind. Yes, you will eventually come back. But it doesn't feel like we are doing it together." Harold confesses how unfair this criticism felt as he thought "So what if I didn't want to do her slow, casual pace the whole bike ride? I did always circle around and come back to her. Why shouldn't I get some rigorous exercise out of this?" He had all kinds of rationalizations.

Dalia continued, "This is just like what goes on in our marriage. For example, in our decision making, you disregard the fact that I need time to process. In your excitement and impatience, you move full speed ahead with implementing whatever grand idea you believe makes sense and not waiting for me to be fully on board." Later, Harold admits that he was sorely missing the point. Yes, Dalia felt left behind while bike riding. But, even more problematic, she felt left behind in the marriage. Instead of working on riding together, those nice matching bikes ended up sitting in a garage for years collecting dust—the unrealized potential to what could have been.

Sadly, this unrealized potential was reflected in our Christian marriage as well. We were doing alright as a couple. But, for years, we struggled as a couple to "ride together" in a way that glorified God.

These past few years of following the Lord in founding our marriage-focused non-profit, Eusebeia, revealed why biking together was such a struggle for us. We had our own separate agendas for what we wanted to get out of the biking experience and the marriage experience. But, the Lord has used Eusebeia to focus us on the Holy Spirit's agenda in our marriage. It hasn't been easy releasing our own agendas in favor of the Lord's agenda. But, here are some of the ways the Holy Spirit eventually captured our attention:

- The Holy Spirit's directive to embody spiritual rather than carnal weapons in our fight for marriage (2 Corinthians 10:3-4) helps us release the selfish attitudes that stunted our growth for years.
- The Holy Spirit's conviction to the practice of spiritual disciplines together like daily devotionals and weekly fasting have honed our sensitivity to better serve one another (1 Timothy 4:7-8).
- The Holy Spirit's challenge to embody the Lord's desires over our own has seriously curbed our wayward, materialistic appetites (Philippians 3:4).

We are now becoming avid listeners of the Holy Spirit. Our marriage is growing at a torrid pace. We are already experiencing touches of abundance. But, the Lord has shown that more is coming—much, much more.

We are experiencing abundance in our marriage (e.g., wisdom, joy, peace, money) that God is harvesting for the uplift of the Kingdom of God. And the books that we author, the non-profit that we direct, and the counseling that we proffer are all vehicles for this abundance.

We have replaced those old Schwinn bikes with newer models. But, it isn't the change in bikes that has mattered most. The riders have changed too. We went out bike riding together last month—side by side, all the way.

Prayer Lesson 10
Pray for Abundance Through Alignment
Amos 9:13

Let's Talk

MONDAY

- Think back over the time you've been married. What has been one thing in your marriage that began with good intentions but actually exposed problems in your relationship together?
- How did this these problems manifest between you? If you've been able to work through those problems, how did you do it? If you haven't been able to work through it, what help do you need?

TUESDAY

- In what areas of your marriage do each of you feel that you have most experienced God's abundance? What does it feel like for you when you know that your marriage is benefiting from the abundance of the Lord?
- In your marriage, when does God's abundance feel distant? What is typically happening when you feel this way? As a couple, how do you find abundance again when it feels lost?

WEDNESDAY

- How do you typically respond when you feel unfairly criticized by your spouse? Does your typical response draw you closer to your spouse or create more distance between you? What can you learn from how Jesus Christ responded when He was unfairly treated?
- In what ways are you unfair (nagging, over stating, inpatient, etc.) in the criticism that you direct towards your spouse? What could you do better?

THURSDAY

- God has a unique agenda for every married couple. What do you believe is God's agenda for your marriage?
- What are the ways that your own personal agendas are making it difficult for God's agenda to rule in your marriage?

FRIDAY

- Your abundant harvest is not mostly for you. Who does God want to bless from the abundance He gives to your marriage?
- What mental limits do you have that inhibits your ability to share God's abundance with a wider circle of people?

Let's Reflect

> Pray for Abundance Through Alignment

As you reflect on this week's lesson and questions, what is God speaking to you as a couple about receiving and sharing His abundance? In the space below, record what you are going to do differently in your marriage.

_____

_____

_____

_____

_____

_____

MONDAY

Dear Lord, we need more of your grace in our marriage. We have done some things well. But, sometimes our good intentions have resulted in negative outcomes. You know our hearts. Forgive us for any selfish motivation. We need your Holy Spirit help to keep us on the path that you have for us. We will do better to heed the directions that you give us. In the name of the Absolute Jesus Christ of Nazareth we pray. Amen.

TUESDAY

Dear Lord, there is nothing greater than resting in your abundance. Your abundance brings peace and joy that strengthen us. Your abundance brings freedom and courage. Your abundance brings opportunities to be generous. Sometimes as a couple, we struggle to keep our eyes focused on your abundance and allow our hearts to be mired in scarcity and doubt. We know this is the Adversary. Forgive us, Lord, for the times we lose faith and trust in your provision. We believe you, Lord. But, please help us in our unbelief. We know that you want to give the keys to the Kingdom to us as we follow you. Our hearts and arms are open to you. In the name of the Absolute Jesus Christ of Nazareth we pray. Amen.

WEDNESDAY

Dear Lord, help us through those times when there is a critical spirit that invades our marriage. The critical spirit divides us with lies that we are not enough. The critical spirit spews blame all over our house. The critical spirit creates confusion and anxiety and depression in our home and it spills out into other areas of our lives. We know that the name of Jesus has the power to subdue this critical spirit. and call on your power and strength to break his yoke. In the name of the Absolute Jesus Christ of Nazareth we pray. Amen.

THURSDAY

Dear Lord, even though we struggle from time to time to keep it in focus, we know that our ultimate desire is to follow your agenda as a couple. Each of us has done things consciously and unconsciously that makes it difficult for your purposes to flow through our marriage. We fall down more than we care to admit. But, we do keep getting up. We pray that your Holy Spirit will continue to convict us when a critical spirit invades our home and that we will obey the directions of the Holy Spirit as to the right action and attitude to display to one another. We pray for the better spiritual discernment and maturity to recognize the Adversary's critical invasion for what it is, and to invoke your name to get us back on track. In the name of the Absolute Jesus Christ of Nazareth we pray. Amen.

FRIDAY

Dear Lord, we know that you don't bless us just for us. Forgive us for all of the ways that we hid and quenched the blessings that were supposed to flow through us to others. We are guilty of storing up your treasure rather than giving it away. Forgive us. We know that scripture teaches that the measure that we give is the same measure that will be used for what we receive. We will open our hearts to spread more of your blessings to those you put in our paths. In the name of the Absolute Jesus Christ of Nazareth we pray. Amen.

PRAY FOR YOUR DELIGHT IN THE LORD

REFERENCE SCRIPTURE

"The Lord directs the steps of the godly. He delights in every detail of their lives."—Psalm 37:23, NLT.

BREATH PRAYER

Touch our hearts so that our greatest desire for our marriage is for you to delight in us.

OBJECT STORY

FINDING MARITAL DIRECTION IN GOD'S DELIGHT

As I (Harold) slowly turned into the long winding driveway, I was expecting to see large welcoming signage informing me of my arrival on the campus of the Blue Mountain Christian Retreat and Conference Center. But, it was much more nondescript than I was anticipating. Though Dalia had been here a couple of times before, this was my first time making the one-and-a-half-hour trip from our home to this retreat center in a rural Pennsylvania town. I couldn't help but ask myself, "Exactly what am I doing here?"

Over the past year and a half, the Lord has directed both of us towards the practice of spiritual disciplines to aid our spiritual formation as a couple. One of the most consistent learnings from this study is the criticality of solitude and silence in creating the space to truly listen for God's voice—in whatever form it takes. Solitude creates that one-on-one experience with God while silence calms the external and internal noise that interferes with our spiritual reception. After more than a year of thinking about it, this short retreat trip was my (Harold's) feeble effort to say, "Lord, here I am".

The polite woman at the registration desk asked, "What brings you here?" I stammered a bit as I tried my best not to just admit, "Honestly, I'm not sure." With room key in hand, I set off for the official (and tepid) start of my "silent retreat."

Once settled into my room with its spartan accommodations, the feeling that I had no idea what I was doing intensified. I reached into my backpack and pulled out the four books that I had brought with me:

Prayer Lesson 11
Pray for Your Delight in the Lord   Psalm 37:23

---

two Bibles (different translations), Ruth Haley Barton's Silence and Solitude, and a mostly empty journal. I plopped down on the somewhat firm, stiff-backed couch and prayed something like, "Lord, I'm here. But, what am I supposed to do during this silent retreat?" I waited and prayed and waited some more. I distinctly remember feeling like an imposter. The negative thoughts swirled in my head. At first, the thoughts were, You don't know what you're doing. You're wasting your time. Then it got worse, You've read all of this stuff about spiritual disciplines and talked to all these people about them. But, after all of this, you still aren't going to hear anything from God. Then, it got even worse, Yes, you've gotten better as a husband. But, it's gotten as good as it's going to get. In one sense, I knew these random thoughts were from the Adversary (that flesh part within me). But, I struggled to quiet the sense of being a fraud.

With doubts swirling, I picked up one of my Bibles and somehow ended up at Psalm 37:23: "The Lord directs the steps of the godly. He delights in every detail of their lives." I re-read the passage dozens of times—each time finding incrementally more peace in its message. The distracting voices in my head quieted. As I focus on the Lord, He in turn directs my steps. As long as I pursue godliness, I have the iron-clad assurance that the Holy Spirit is guiding my steps. As long as my eyes remain on the Father, the Lord will orchestrate my actions as a husband in pursuit of a marriage that pleases Him. I scribbled some notes in my journal. I remember telling myself, "I am here on this silent retreat under the direction of the Lord." Despite my lack of clarity about what I should do or expect from this silent retreat, I could feel certain that each minute here was ordained by God.

I spent almost the entire night studying Psalm 37 including its powerful fourth verse, "Take delight in the Lord and he will give you your heart's desires." As I delight in Him, his steps become my heart's desires. And, He delights in my life's every detail—even the moments of uncertainty.

children, bills, and ministry demands so that you pursue a marriage that pleases you more than one that pleases the Lord. But, may I encourage you to find space for solitude and silence (even thirty minutes once or twice a week) to fight through your own external and internal noise that burdens your marriage. Solitude and silence are the points of breakthrough to the next level of godliness in your marriage because it is there that you discover the Lord's delight. Be encouraged today that the Lord directs the steps of the godly and is waiting to take delight in your every detail.

Prayer Lesson 11
Pray for Your Delight in the Lord — Psalm 37:23

Let's Talk

MONDAY

- With what frequency do each of you spend alone time with God? When alone with the Lord, how much time do you spend with God?
- How often do the two of you get away for a private retreat with God as a couple? Plan a spiritual couple retreat where just the two of you spend time sharing with each other and listening to God without any distractions (e.g., children, television, internet surfing).

TUESDAY

- In what ways and how frequently have you practiced deliberate times of silence with God in your own spiritual formation as individuals and as a couple?
- What steps do you each need to take to set aside regular times of silence with God to listen for His direction for your marriage?

WEDNESDAY

- As a couple, do you ever feel like spiritual imposters when you struggle with growing Christlike in your marriage? How do you push through this 'imposter syndrome' in order to grow closer to the Lord?
- What negative thoughts constantly swirl in your head about your spouse and your marriage? How do you replace the negativity with love and redemptive self-talk?

THURSDAY

- The featured scripture this week assures us that the Lord delights in the details of your marriage. In what particular details of your marriage are you confident that the Lord delights?
- As you think about God's work in your marriage, how are you experiencing and sharing delight in what God is doing?

FRIDAY

- Psalm 37:4 instructs us that delighting in the Lord is one path to receiving the desires of your heart. As you have reflected and prayed about the ways in which you delight in the Lord as a couple, what have you learned about the desires of your heart?
- There is power in agreement. As a couple, which godly desires are God stirring in you both that reveal the nature of His unique work in your marriage?

Psalm 37:23

Let's Reflect

Pray for Your Delight in the Lord

This week your reflections and prayers focus on delight as a guide for God's direction in your marriage. As you reflect on this week's lesson and questions, think about the details of your marriage—the way you show love to one another, communication styles, household chores, parenting responsibilities, sexual intimacy. In the space below, record in what details you have seen the most progress towards Christlikeness, and what details continue to be a struggle for you as a couple. Brainstorm and record a few ideas to spend more time delighting in the Lord as a couple.

Prayer Lesson 11
Pray for Your Delight in the Lord

Psalm 37:23

Let's Pray

MONDAY

Dear Lord, busyness has become a badge of respect in our culture. As a couple, we have too often replaced the tireless pursuit of you with a tiring pursuit of achievements and things that make us feel good for a short period of time. For one reason or another, we have not prioritized time alone with you either as individuals or as a couple. And, this lapse shows in the struggles we have with communication, working together as a team, and having the influence for the Kingdom of God that we know you intend for us. Give us the courage to set aside things that distract us from spending personal time with you and listening for your direction. In the name of the Absolute Jesus Christ of Nazareth we pray. Amen.

TUESDAY

Dear Lord, we are overwhelmed by noise everywhere in our lives. We have grown accustomed to being inundated with noise and have forgotten how silence sounds. We need to create spaces where we can be alone with you without any other distractions. But, we keep making excuses and our spiritual life suffers as a result. We need the conviction of your Holy Spirit to direct us to areas where your still, small voice can be heard. We will make this space a priority. In the name of the Absolute Jesus Christ of Nazareth we pray. Amen.

WEDNESDAY

Dear Lord, it is difficult to stay positive about our marriage when we are struggling to find a good spiritual rhythm as a couple. Honestly, sometimes, we just get tired of trying because it seems that we just keep going in circles and getting nowhere fast. It feels easier just to live our married lives each in our own lane rather than sharing the lane together. We feel like imposters more often then we should. Despite all of these challenges, we believe that you have not given up on us. You are still pointing us to pick up our cross and follow you. It is the sacrifice we make for the cross that holds the promise for a better marriage for us. In the name of the Absolute Jesus Christ of Nazareth we pray. Amen.

THURSDAY

Dear Lord, in your omniscience, you know every detail of our marriage just like the Apostle Luke (Luke 12:7) tells us you know the number of hairs on our head. While every detail is not pretty or righteous between us as a couple, we are confident that we are growing more like Christ as we commit the details to Him. You know our hearts. And, our hearts delight in your laws and in your presence. Help us to keep focusing on your presence in the details of our marriage. In the name of the Absolute Jesus Christ of Nazareth we pray. Amen.

FRIDAY

Dear Lord, there is no greater goal for us as a couple than to be the object of your affection and delight. We know that as your children you love us unconditionally. But, we also know that we have thought and done many things in which you would not take delight. We err when we put our own pleasure before your delight. May your Holy Spirit continue to purge our human nature and replace it with your divine nature so that we submit all of the details of our marriage to you and delight in you as you delight in us. In the name of the Absolute Jesus Christ of Nazareth we pray. Amen.

PRAY FOR AGAPE LOVE

REFERENCE SCRIPTURE

"In fact, though by this time you ought to be teachers, you need someone to teach you the elementary truths of God's word all over again. You need milk, not solid food! Anyone who lives on milk, being still an infant, is not acquainted with the teaching about righteousness. But solid food is for the mature, who by constant use have trained themselves to distinguish good from evil."
—Hebrews 5:12-14, NIV.

BREATH PRAYER

May the indwelling of the Holy Spirit and its work through us enlarge our territory as a couple.

OBJECT STORY
CHRIST OVER CREDENTIALS

We love graduation celebrations because they recognize the achievement that comes with staying consistent with one's goal. Graduation parties are wonderful celebrations filled with balloons, cards, family, and well-wishers. But, behind all the pomp and circumstance is the achievement of a person who stayed committed.

At this point, you may be wondering, "Why is Team Arnold talking about graduation in a marriage story?" We have been married for more than three decades, but we're a long way from graduation when it comes to spiritual truths. Honestly, for much of our marriage, we have demonstrated only an elementary understanding of Christlikeness. How can so many of us be married for decades and still be spiritually in primary school? It's the same reason the Hebrew people wandered in the desert for forty years, unable to reach the land God promised them. We refuse godliness.

Together, one or both of us, has served as minister, published author of multiple marriage books, and marriage educators. We have six degrees and one biblical certification between us, including a Master's degree in Marriage and Family Therapy from a world-renown seminary and a doctorate in psychology. We have counseled couples for more than fifteen years. In all these roles, we have considered ourselves called by the Lord to this endeavor and aspired to operate in conjunction with the Holy Spirit. So what's the point? We have all of the academic and ministerial credentials to be a Christlike husband and wife...but for most of more than three and a half decades of marriage, we haven't been very Christlike as spouses. It's not about credentials. It's about Christ.

Prayer Lesson 12
Pray for Agape Love

Hebrews 5:12-14

While having all of the credentials, we have not always asked ourselves these questions, or acted on them:
- How does our tone of voice reflect Christ?
- How does our generosity (of time, attention, and resources) with each other reflect Christ?
- How does our humility with each other reflect Christ?
- How does our patience with each other reflect Christ?
- How much time do we spend together worshiping Christ?

Of course, we love each other; we've loved each other since we started dating in college. But we've loved each other with an insufficient kind of love—our love (secular love) more than Christ's love (spiritual love). How do you know which love you are showing your spouse? Secular love comes from within you. It is usually conditional. It is usually temporal (limited in time and space). And, it is usually self-serving. On the other hand, spiritual love comes from the Lord. It is always agape and unconditional. It is always eternal (lasting into eternity). And it is always spouse-serving. But, here is the difficulty. It is impossible to practice spouse-serving spiritual love with a self-serving carnal heart. How can you practice spiritual love in this type of marriage that often feels anything but spiritual?

To practice spiritual love is to love like Christ with forgiveness and grace. But, you cannot do this of your own will. Spiritual love is only possible through the grace and forgiveness that comes with sanctification—for the individual and the marriage. Spiritual love is not about perfection but the pursuit of perfect holiness. We've come to increasingly understand over the past several years that spiritual love is less about us per se, and more about each of us in service to Christ through the pursuit of sanctification. The Adversary wants us to see love as something that we earn or deserve. Christ wants us to see love as His gift to us.

As a believer in the Lord Jesus Christ, God has written your name in the Lamb's book of life. But, you still need more than an elementary spirituality to experience the Kingdom of God in your marriage or to maximize your outreach with the gospel through your marriage. Your best ministry demands that you practice Christlikeness day in and day out. It's time for you and us to graduate from the amateur marriage ranks and be the professional ministers of the gospel through our marriages.

Prayer Lesson 12
Pray for Agape Love

Hebrews 5:12-14

Let's Talk

MONDAY
- Would you describe your marriage as it stands today as defined more by spiritual meat or milk? Explain.
- What do each of you need to do to deepen the spiritual meat of your marriage?

TUESDAY
- How can academic and ministry credentials actually impede your growth as a couple towards Christlikeness?
- How can credentials be helpful in your journey together towards Christ? Are there credentials to which you aspire?

WEDNESDAY
- How well does your tone of voice, generosity, humility, patience, and quality of time together as a couple reflect Christ? Which needs the most work?
- How can your sacrifice for Christ deepen your love for your spouse?

THURSDAY
- What does it take from each of you on a daily basis to replace secular love with spiritual love in your marriage?
- What needs to shift inside each of you to more consistently demonstrate agape or unconditional love to your spouse?

FRIDAY
- What would you be doing to demonstrate love toward each other that would present a more mature leven of sanctification?
- What do you believe a sanctified version of each of you means to those who are watching you?

Let's Reflect

Pray for Agape Love

This week, your reflections and prayers are about moving from secular love to spiritual love as your marriage becomes sanctified. Each of you are to record three ways that the Lord is calling you to a deeper level of sanctification as a spouse. As you move towards this vision for sanctification, what is God going to make possible for your marriage? What doors do you want God to open for you as a couple?

Prayer Lesson 12
Pray for Agape Love

Hebrews 5:12-14

Let's Pray

MONDAY

Dear Lord, you give us grace to grow. You want us to demonstrate the spiritual meat that the Apostle Paul talks about in 1 Corinthians chapter 3. You give us growth opportunities because you love us and desire the best for us. But, those opportunities are almost always on the other side of challenges that you place or allow in our path. Thank you for caring enough about us to not always give us what we want, but what we need. Growth means that our marriage values holiness more than happiness. As we embody spiritual meat as a couple, we are helping other couples in their own marriages. As they experience our repentance for immature words and deeds, they can see the powerful transformation that comes with being a child of God. We are blessed to have you drawing us towards the meat of marriage. In the name of the Absolute Jesus Christ of Nazareth we pray. Amen.

TUESDAY

Dear Lord, elevation in the Kingdom of God comes from you. It has been tempting sometimes to look for praise from family and friends. It has been tempting to compare ourselves with other couples. There have been times when we failed to value each other. And, that devaluation has hurt our marriage. But, we see more clearly now. We see that only what we do for Christ will last. We know that you tell us that if all our elevation happens on earth then we are robbing ourselves of heavenly rewards. We want the heavenly rewards that await us. Help us to keep our sights on eternal gains while practicing the behaviors that grow us towards you and one another here on earth. In the name of the Absolute Jesus Christ of Nazareth we pray. Amen.

WEDNESDAY

Dear Lord, we say that we love you. But, our marriage doesn't always reflect that love. We say that we love each other. But, many of our actions run counter to what love actually means. We have used the word 'love' too lightly because it is cliché to say it. Despite our many misses, we are committed to more depth in our love and commitment to one another. We don't only want to love one another, but we want to like each other as well. For us, the maturity from spiritual milk to meat is about being friends that serve one another. We are friends of God and friends as spouses. We believe God smiles on that fact as the only credential that really matters. In the name of the Absolute Jesus Christ of Nazareth we pray. Amen.

THURSDAY

Dear Lord, it is impossible to practice spouse-serving spiritual love with a self-serving heart. Spiritual love begins with you and is impossible outside of you. Spiritual love always reveals truth and is impossible without centering you as the Truth in our marriage. We are tired of the limits and empty promises of secular love in our marriage. We are tired of the hypocrisy that we feel when we think about the desires of our flesh (selfishness, impatience, unforgiveness). You have more for us than our flesh can even understand. We can only fathom the beauty of spiritual love (grace, forgiveness, self-control) as we release the expectations that this love is to serve us. We must serve love—to you and to one another. In the name of the Absolute Jesus Christ of Nazareth we pray. Amen.

Prayer Lesson 12
Pray for Agape Love — Hebrews 5:12-14

FRIDAY

Dear Lord, the message of the Kingdom of God is two-fold—salvation and sanctification. As Christian couples, we have often focused, rightly so, on the importance of salvation through Jesus Christ. As a couple, we each call him Lord and savior. The challenge, however, is sanctification. Salvation is the beginning, not the ending. The work of marriage lies in its sanctification—becoming more Christ-like. We have much work to do to look more like Christ as husbands and wives. We will become the models of sanctification that you have ordained for us. We will not settle for less. Salvation is beautiful. But, it is only part of your work for us. We surrender ourselves to the work of sanctification. In the name of the Absolute Jesus Christ of Nazareth we pray. Amen.

PRAY FOR GRACEFUL INFLUENCE

REFERENCE SCRIPTURE

"Follow me as I follow Christ", -1 Corinthians 11:1, MEV.

BREATH PRAYER

May we walk together with such a divine and unique anointing that those watching us ask us how they can grow in relationship with Christ.

OBJECT STORY
A GREAT MARRIAGE THAT NEVER WAS

For Dalia and me, 2021 was the most fascinating and exciting of more than thirty years of marriage. During a global pandemic (COVID-19) when so many homes and relationships ruptured, Dalia and I discovered our best season of marriage—the way it was supposed to be for the past three decades, but somehow never was. In a way, it's like we're honeymooning again—but this time motivated more by a mutual desire for pleasing God more than pleasing ourselves. The odd thing is that we've always believed that we had a great marriage. A cursory glance at our 'marriage resume' seems to support this belief. We've led hundreds of marriage workshops and classes, published marriage books and articles, led marriage ministry for our local church, counseled countless Christian couples, raised two godly children to adulthood, and most of the time identified as a 'happy' couple. Yet today, the Holy Spirit is showing us the very sobering reality that our marriage reeked with spiritual immaturity—offensive to God's nostrils. Our marriage was not what the Apostle Paul describes to the Corinthian Church as 'the aroma of Christ to God' (2 Corinthians 2:15).

We started the Eusebeia non-profit organization in 2017 with this conviction to be obedient to the Lord in leading a spiritual revival for Christian marriage. In those first several years, it felt like a fuzzy goal with little practical guidance. What neither of us realized when we started the non-profit is that, even after many years of marriage, we did not know how to follow Christ as a couple. Sure, we are both Holy Spirit-filled. We are both active, committed, tithe-paying leaders in the church. We are both anointed with spiritual gifts that bless the Kingdom of God. In other words, we individually performed Kingdom works, yet our marriage was not transformed by them. How does that happen? It happens because our ability to follow is deeply flawed. We don't know how to systematically follow the Holy Spirit that Christ sent to lead us.

Our mindsets are corrupted by the 'follow ideology' of the secular world that idolizes pleasure. My ego says, 'follow me.'. My social media profile says, 'follow me.' My ministry branding says, 'follow me.' The more others follow, the more successful and happier I feel. In a real sense, far too many of us calculate our life's worth by who follows us.

There is, however, another way. In 1 Corinthians 11:1, the Apostle Paul offers the divine perspective on what it means to follow. It is this passage that has charted a new path in marriage for us over the past year and a half. It says simply, "Follow me as I follow Christ" (MEV). In our marriage, rather than focusing on whether or not each of us is following the other, we need to focus on how well we are truly following Christ. Following Christ demands personal sacrifice and humility. Following Christ means gracefully loving each other in our strengths and weaknesses. Following Christ means embracing holiness as a lifestyle. We know all of these things in our head. But, we don't embrace it in our heart.

We have a long way to go on this path to a spiritually mature marriage that is more favored than flawed. But, here is what we can confidently say to your marriage, "Follow us as we follow Christ." We are doing our best to live out the spiritual disciplines in our home. Our goal is to be participants in a spiritual revival for Christian marriage by inviting you to follow us—but only as far as we follow Christ.

Your marriage will not find its true identity until you spend more time as a couple in prayer and fasting together as a marriage team. God's magnificence is only manifest as you follow as one flesh.

Prayer Lesson 13
Pray for Graceful Influence

1 Corinthians 11:1

Let's Talk

MONDAY
- How sober are you about the true state of your marriage today? What aroma does your marriage leave in God's nostrils?
- How confident are you that you know how to follow Christ as a couple?

TUESDAY
- In what, if any, ways is your busyness masking the difficulty you are having in following Christ's Word as a couple?
- What do people who know you see in your marriage, and how does that compare to what you see? If there is a gap between the two, what heart surgery does the Lord need to perform in each of you in order to decrease that gap?

WEDNESDAY
- Honestly, as individuals and a couple, do you focus more on who is following you or how you are following Christ?
- Are you walking in such a way that your spouse can trust following you? What struggles do you have in following your spouse's leading?

THURSDAY
- Read Ephesians 5:21 together. What specific attitudes and behaviors must shift in your marriage for you to be mutually submissive to each other as the Apostle Paul instructs?
- The ability to follow is contingent on the ability to listen. What are your strengths and weaknesses in listening to one another as a couple? How often do you feel truly heard by your spouse?

FRIDAY
- Can you sincerely invite other couples to follow your marriage as you follow Christ? Share your rationale with each other.
- What one thing can you do differently that will make the invitation to follow you more God-honoring?

Let's Reflect

> Pray for Graceful Influence

This week, your reflections and prayers center around what it means to follow. The ability to follow is a fundamental building block of Christlikeness. In several scriptures, Jesus Christ instructed others to pick up their cross and follow Him (Matthew 4:18-20, John 10:27). Following Christ together as a couple requires humility and a desire to listen well to Him and to one another. In your journal, write how the Holy Spirit reveals that you each can become better listeners.

_____

_____

_____

_____

_____

_____

Prayer Lesson 13
Pray for Graceful Influence — 1 Corinthians 11:1

Let's Pray

MONDAY

Dear Lord, thank you for shining a light on the soul of our marriage and looking into the nooks and crannies of our union. Thank you for the Holy Spirit's conviction that we feel in our spirit when we stray from your Word. With conviction comes the opportunity for redemption. Conviction is your grace and a reminder that you hold our marriage in the palm of your hands. Even in our flaws you show us favor. Forgive us for the big and small ways that we keep running roughshod over that which you instructed us to hold dear. Help us to slow our lives and our minds so that we can stay present in the moments that matter in our marriage. In the name of the Absolute Jesus Christ of Nazareth we pray. Amen.

TUESDAY

Dear Lord, man sees the outward appearance but you see the heart. You know the heart that we each bring to this marriage each day. You are not fooled by pretense and superficial posturing. You hold us accountable for what happens inside us. You hate hypocrisy. You want us to be honest about the good, the bad, and the ugly. The good is that we know that your Holy Spirit indwells us and keeps drawing us to be better than we were yesterday. The bad news is that we keep falling into disobedience and operating from our flesh rather than from your spirit within us. The ugly news is that we allowed the Adversary to use us to harm one another. We are sorry for the bad and the ugly things we have done. But, we are going to keep working to allow more of the good news in our life together because you are the good news within us. In the name of the Absolute Jesus Christ of Nazareth we pray. Amen.

WEDNESDAY

Dear Lord, we are flawed as followers. We follow people and pursuits that satisfy the desires of our flesh more than we follow your Holy Word. We cannot follow these worldly influences and you at the same time. Help us to discern when our hearts are following after the wrong things. As a husband and wife, help us work together to stay accountable to each other in following you. We know that your Word in Ephesians chapter 5 encourages us to submit ourselves to one another. Help us to follow that instruction. We know that you've ordained husbands to take the mantle of servant leadership in marriage. We know that you've ordained wives to work in partnership with their husbands. Transform our flawed attitudes about submission so that you get the glory in how we follow you. In the name of the Absolute Jesus Christ of Nazareth we pray.

THURSDAY

Dear Lord, until we each learn to follow the instruction of your Word, we will never understand your desire for us as a couple. Help us to uphold your Word as the absolute, not a relative Truth. Help us to discern the still, small voice of your Holy Spirit over the clatter of our noisy culture. Help us to find righteous people whose example we can follow. We are learning that we can only follow scripture as we listen for the heart of Christ's message that it extends. We are learning that we can only follow your Holy Spirit as we follow Galatians 5:25 and keep in step with the Spirit. We are learning that we can only follow righteous people that you place in our lives. We have not been great listeners as a couple. But, that is changing now. In the name of the Absolute Jesus Christ of Nazareth we pray. Amen.

FRIDAY

Dear Lord, our marriage has often not been in a favored posture with you. We still have a lot of work to do. But, we believe that you honor our desire and efforts to seek you first. As our marriage continues on this path towards greater Christlikeness, you give us permission to invite others to follow us—not in our perfection but in your promise. You promise that you will withhold nothing from us and that you will make beauty from ashes. You promise that you will never leave or forsake us. Those and so many more promises are what keep us going, especially through the difficult days. We are being made perfect in you. And, that is exactly what we are asking other people to follow. Follow us as we follow Christ. In the name of the Absolute Jesus Christ of Nazareth we pray. Amen.

PRAY FOR SELF-DENIAL

REFERENCE SCRIPTURE

"Whoever wants to be my disciple must deny themselves and take up their cross daily and follow me.",—Luke 9:23, KJV.

BREATH PRAYER

Purify our minds so that we will deny ourselves and pick up the cross you have for us and constantly choose to follow you together.

OBJECT STORY
THE MARRIED ROAD LESS TRAVELLED

Lent is an important time of year because it sets the stage for the most significant event in the history of the Church—the death and resurrection of our Lord and Savior, Jesus Christ—Easter. The lent season is about self-denial. Why self-denial? Jesus speaks directly to this fundamental question: "Whoever wants to be my disciple must deny themselves and take up their cross daily and follow me" (Luke 9:23, KJV). Jesus' words cannot be clearer. You must experience lent to embrace Easter. All of us say that we want to be Christ's disciple. What we really want to do is what the rich young ruler wanted to do when he confronted Jesus (Luke 18:18-23). We want to have it both ways. We love Jesus and want to follow Jesus. But, we don't love or trust him enough to let go of the security and pleasures we enjoy.

Theologian Dietrich Bonhoeffer famously coined the term 'cheap grace' to describe the watered-down version of Christianity we embrace, a faith which is ultimately no Christianity at all because it lacks homage to the true nature of Jesus Christ. Our fear is that we as a community of Christian couples have embraced 'cheap discipleship' that doesn't require a commitment to the spiritual disciplines. 'Cheap discipleship' has no theological foundation because there is no true Jesus in it. 'Cheap discipleship' is self-worship rather than self-denial.

If we want to follow Jesus we must come to grips with self-denial on a daily basis. This is not easy. The first disciples of Jesus had to drop everything they knew, leave their jobs, and live an itinerant lifestyle away from their families. But, Jesus is asking the same level of sacrifice from us today. He probably isn't asking you to leave your job and family to follow Him. But, He is definitely insisting that you deny yourself each day to do so.

Deny yourself the right to be selfish, unforgiving, self-righteous, and in control. And, it should begin in your most sacred human relationship—your marriage.

When Jesus tells you to take up your cross daily, He dispels the myth of 'cheap discipleship' because He knows that it is only by God's grace that any of us persist in self-denial. The real beauty, however, of self-denial is that it leaves a cup for God to fill with anointed oil.

Herein lies the absolute miracle of marriage. For the Christian couple who commits to self-denial, you release your spiritual DNA as a couple. Your spiritual DNA is the genotype or blueprint that distinguishes your divine purpose from every other couple in the Kingdom of God. It is the anointed cup that God overflows so that your marriage lifts Him up and draws everyone that sees you towards Him.

As much as the evidence of 'cheap discipleship' is praised in our Christian culture, it is a distortion of the Father of Lies. We are only disciples of the Absolute Christ when we choose each day to pick up that cross of self-denial—especially when it feels heavy. We'll leave you with these closing words to poet Robert Frost's classic poem, "The Road Not Taken."

"Two roads diverged in a wood, and I—
I took the one less traveled by,
And that has made all the difference."

Prayer Lesson 14
Pray for Self-Denial

Luke 9:23

Let's Talk

MONDAY
- Why is self-denial important to walking with Christ in marriage?
- How easily does self-denial come to each of you in your marriage? Share a recent example when you embodied self-denial in your marriage

TUESDAY
- What does Christian spiritual formation (the journey of becoming more Christ-like for the sake of others) look like in your lives?
- What will it take for your marriage to consistently represent Christian discipleship?

WEDNESDAY
- For each of you, how is the struggle with self-denial most destructive in your marriage?
- How, if at all, do your actions cheapen the grace that God shows you as a couple?

THURSDAY
- What is the spiritual DNA (also known as 'the anointing') of your marriage? If it isn't obvious to you, you may need to ask others who know you well.
- How are you living out your marriage's anointing? To what is God calling your anointing?

FRIDAY
- What does Christ's resurrection mean for the anointing and purpose that you have as a couple?
- One day, you will each stand before God at that great Judgment Day. What do each of you want God to say about how your marriage served as part of your sanctification?

Let's Reflect

> Pray for Self-Denial

This week, your reflections and prayers ground in spiritual disciplines that form your marriage in the image of Christ. Spiritual formation always begins with refusing to worship the self. Based on your reflections this week, what is the anointing that God (through the Holy Spirit) is shaping in you as a couple? List some specific ways that you sense the Holy Spirit desires to manifest in that marital anointing. If you are struggling to identify your anointing together, then think about your individual areas of gifting and talent (what comes easily for you) and imagine ways that these individual strengths could work together. If you still struggle, ask 2-3 other spirit-led people that know you well as a couple, "When you think about us as a married couple, how do you see God manifest Himself through us?"

_____

_____

_____

_____

_____

Prayer Lesson 14
Pray for Self-Denial

Luke 9:23

Let's Pray

MONDAY

Dear Lord, how many times have we tried to walk with you without letting go of our own desires? How many times have we tried to have it both ways—be righteous and selfish at the same time? How many times have we cried out to you for help without being obedient to what you've already asked of us? How many times have we fallen down in our walk towards Christlikeness? These are all too numerous to count. But the bigger question is, how many times we have gotten back up and tried again? We cannot thank you enough because every time we fall down, you give us the strength to get back up and try again. We probably will fall again. But, we will never stop getting up together. In the name of the Absolute Jesus Christ of Nazareth we pray. Amen.

TUESDAY

Dear Lord, we are a couple of faith and our marriage is Spirit-driven. We want to grow our faith so that our marriage is worthy of the investment that you want to make in us. We want to grow in grace so that we abandon legalism and humanism in our marriage. We want your glory cloud to rest above our home such that all who enter our residence feel a personal touch from you. We want the Adversary to know that he isn't welcome in our sacred home. This type of relationship with you comes from being continually shaped by immersion in your Word, in silence and solitude, in prayer and fasting, and in community with faithful others. Help our marriage grow as a disciple of your Kingdom. In the name of the Absolute Jesus Christ of Nazareth we pray. Amen.

WEDNESDAY

Dear Lord, without self-denial, we cannot know you. The Adversary lies to us through self-promotion. He wants us to worship the self. This is the hallmark of idolatry. You will have no one or no thing be worshipped but you. Forgive us for the sin of idolatry that has happened with our selfishness. We are tearing down the altars of the self in our marriage. We are purging our temples. From this day forward, we declare that our bodies are temples of the Living God refreshed by your Living Water. Selfishness has no place here. In the name of the Absolute Jesus Christ of Nazareth we pray. Amen.

THURSDAY

Dear Lord, your Holy Spirit has encoded its imprint in our marriage. The imprint of the Holy Spirit is our anointing and points the way to our calling as a team of two. Our anointing helps us know what ministry and service opportunities to which we should say 'yes'. Conversely, knowing our anointing helps us filter out the things to which you're directing us to say 'no'. Yes, we are each individually valued by the Lord. We each have an anointing. But, as a couple, we have our own anointing together. And, we are called to share that anointing in unique ways in service to the King of Kings. In the name of the Absolute Jesus Christ of Nazareth we pray. Amen.

FRIDAY

Dear Lord, thank you for dying for our sins. Thank you for sacrificing yourself on Calvary's cross for our marriage. Thank you for enduring the suffering and shame, though we are the ones who deserved it. Thank you for all the ways that you cover the sins of our marriage in the eyes of God the Father.We love you even though we often fail you. Our failures remind us more than ever that this is why you died. In the name of the Absolute Jesus Christ of Nazareth we pray. Amen.

PRAY FOR PREPAREDNESS FOR SPIRITUAL WARFARE

REFERENCE SCRIPTURE

"For those who live according to the flesh set their minds on the things of the flesh, but those who live according to the Spirit set their minds on the things of the Spirit.",—Romans 8:5, NKJV.

BREATH PRAYER

As a couple after your heart, may we be encouraged that there are always more for us than against us.

OBJECT STORY
CHOOSE YOUR HILL

At the end of 2019, we felt this tug in our spirit about a single word: war. It felt heavy in our souls. But, we didn't know why. Of course, neither of us had any idea the COVID-19 pandemic was coming. But, God knew. God has been working within us to better grasp what it means to engage in spiritual warfare beyond just giving it lip service. What does it really mean in the spiritual realm to refuse carnal weapons? As Christ-followers, we always talk about "spiritual warfare." But, we fear that we keep bringing "a knife to a gunfight." Am I really prepared for the fight?

The Bible describes in 1 Samuel (chapter 17) that the Israelite army occupied one hill and the Philistines occupied the other hill with a valley in between them. Scripture proceeds to tell us that King Saul and the Israelite army drew a battle line to war with the Philistines (verse 2). What does it mean to draw the battle line? It means that you are ready to start fighting. It means that the main points of the conflict are clear and everyone knows which side of the line they are on. Yet, upon hearing Goliath's ultimatum the entire Israelite army was "dismayed and terrified" (verse 11). The irony is this: The Israelites had drawn a battle line, but they were not really ready for the fight. The lesson is simple. Anyone can draw a battle line. But, not everyone is prepared to fight.

As we gripped hands in prayer on Good Friday evening during the 2020 pandemic, we thanked God for sacrificing His Son Jesus so that anyone could approach the Holy of Holies and be cleansed (Forgiveness). We thanked God for allowing anyone to be converted from fighting for the forces of darkness to fighting for the forces of the light (Redemption). We found ourselves thanking God for how the resurrection of His Son unequivocally guarantees that we believers win the fight for eternal security (Salvation).

Prayer Lesson 15
Pray for Preparedness for Spiritual Warfare Romans 8:5

As depicted in the 1 Samuel passage earlier, there are still two armies occupying two hills with a valley between them. On one hill stand those who live according to the spirit—defined by their chosen obedience to the Holy Spirit's prompting. On the other hill stand those who live according to the flesh in that they fail to listen or submit to the Holy Spirit's guidance. We make the choice every single day, every single minute as to which hill we choose. For us Christ followers, we have a responsibility to keep choosing the right hill. When you make your absolute best effort to treat your spouse like Christ treats the Church, you choose the right hill. When you give to your neighbor, you choose the right hill. When you prioritize spiritual over material things, you choose the right hill.

Conversely, any time you fail to choose the right hill, you align yourself (at least for a time) with the dark forces that dominate the other hill. When we disobey the Holy Spirit within us, we are choosing darkness over light. We love the words of our friend and pastor in Philadelphia, Dr. Crawford Clark: "You can be in the Church but not in the battle"—or as we may add, "not on the right hill for battle." This is the somber reality of the war we fight.

Today, we are rejoicing because Christ's ultimate sacrifice on a hill called Calvary empowers me each day to choose the right hill too. Christ's victory over death on Resurrection Sunday assures us that even when we err and choose the wrong hill for a time that we will never exhaust His love or his grace. As for our house, we see the battle line and we choose to live and die on the right hill. We pray that this beautiful war story encourages and empowers you to make that same choice.

Let's Talk

MONDAY
- How did the COVID-19 pandemic affect your marriage? Share why you became closer or more distant?
- How much do you share with each other about those times you feel the Holy Spirit's tug within you? Are you comfortable with your answers?

TUESDAY
- If you're being honest, have you ever felt in your own battle as a couple with the Adversary that you were outmatched? Share your thoughts with each other.
- What is your strategy as a team of two to defeat the Adversary when he attacks your marriage?

WEDNESDAY
- This week's object story talks about drawing a battle line. What battle lines have you recently drawn together against the Adversary?
- With the battle line drawn, how prepared are you to fight for righteousness?

THURSDAY
- What strategies and tactics do you employ so that both of you stay on the Lord's side of the battle line?
- What friends and/or family members can you count on to line up with your marriage in opposition to the Adversary's attack?

FRIDAY
- What transgressions do you need the blood of Christ to redeem in your marriage?
- In 2 Corinthians 10:5, the Apostle Paul encourages us to "take every thought captive" in obedience to Christ. What negative thoughts need to be taken captive? How can you work on this together?

Prayer Lesson 15
Pray for Preparedness for Spiritual Warfare

Romans 8:5

Let's Reflect

> Pray for Preparedness for Spiritual Warfare

This week, your reflections and prayers ask you to draw a spiritual 'line in the sand' between your desires for godliness and the Adversary's desire for selfishness. In your journal this week, write a few ideas as to how you can work together as a team to take the offensive against the Adversary and take back territory that he has stolen from your marriage.

_____

_____

_____

_____

_____

_____

Let's Pray

MONDAY

Dear Lord, we want to remember you as "the Risen One." We are thankful for the innocent blood that you shed so that our marriage can stay in right relationship with God, the Father. But, we also want to remember the empty tomb. We want to meditate on how you took victory away from Satan and the grave. The Adversary thought he had defeated you. But your resurrection reminds us that death has no sting and the grave no victory as we stay rooted in you. Your victory means our marriage is victorious over Satan's attacks too. We are not afraid of the battle with him because we know that we have you on our side. You have never lost a battle. You are our champion. In the name of the Absolute Jesus Christ of Nazareth we pray. Amen.

TUESDAY

Dear Lord, your Word (1 Peter 5:8) tells us that Satan is prowling and roaring like a lion looking for whom he may devour. But, you have not given us a spirit of fear but of power, love, and a sound mind. You tell us in that same passage to stay sober-minded and alert so that we can see the enemy for who and what he is. We ask for your wisdom and discernment to know his lies and to make sure the perimeter of our marriage stays impenetrable to his attacks. The Adversary can roar all he likes. But, he can only do what you allow him to do. As we stay rooted and grounded in your Word, we feel assured that no harm will befall us that is too much for us to bear. Thank you for being our sword and shield enabling us to take the offense and defense against his attacks. In the name of the Absolute Jesus Christ of Nazareth we pray. Amen.

WEDNESDAY

Dear Lord, we hate Satan. He has destroyed the lives of so many of our family and friends. We have personally seen how he deceives us by trying to change the narrative to suit his own evil ends. He tries to get us finger pointing at each other rather than him. He wants us to think that we are each other's enemy. He wants us to focus on superficial things rather than eternal things. He wants us to forget that we are fearfully and wonderfully made in you. He wants us to forget that he is a defeated foe. But, we will not forget. Our prayers are to remember exactly him as the father of lies that he is. There is no truth in him. We stand on the hill of Truth because this is where your light overpowers his darkness. Thank you, Lord, for the wisdom in this revelation. In the name of the Absolute Jesus Christ of Nazareth we pray. Amen.

THURSDAY

Dear Lord, great is your faithfulness to us. From the rising of the sun to its setting, your name is worthy to be praised. We praise you for being God, Alpha, our Creator, Immanuel, Abba, Almighty Counselor, Prince of Peace, Everlasting Father, Righteous Judge, Ancient of Days, and Omega. We don't say your many names enough because they are great reminders of all of the ways that you give to us and care for us—in ways we do not at all deserve. But, the name that we always want ready on the tip of our tongues is the name of Jesus because it is only through the name of Jesus that we have access to the Father as individuals and as a couple. The name of Jesus is the name above all names because only through Him can we be redemptive to each other as spouses. Only through Jesus can we forgive the transgressions against one another. Only through Jesus can we extend grace in spite of the hurt. So, we will keep lifting the name of Jesus on the hills and in the valleys. We are not and will never be ashamed of that name. In the name of the Absolute Jesus Christ of Nazareth we pray. Amen.

FRIDAY

Dear Lord, this Christian walk is a battlefield of the mind. As a couple, it is a battlefield of two minds. It's tough enough when there is a battle in one of our minds. But, it's multiplied when we both are wrestling to bring all our thoughts under the subjection of the Holy Spirit. Thankfully, even with our sometimes-divided mind, we follow that one spirit—the Holy Spirit that indwells us. We want the Holy Spirit to transform our minds, as the Apostle Paul tells us to "renew our minds." To renew our minds is to take control of the battlefield. In our humanity, our minds will always be the battleground of the spirit versus the flesh. But, with our renewed minds, the spirit maintains the upper hand. We want a renewed mind about our marriage. We want to see how we must die so that your ultimate desire for us can live. We ask that your desire be resurrected in our minds so that your Holy Spirit can use us to your glory and honor. In the name of the Absolute Jesus Christ of Nazareth we pray. Amen.

PRAY FOR SELFLESS LOVE

REFERENCE SCRIPTURE

"For the love of Christ controls us, because we have concluded this: that ONE has died for all, therefore all have died; and he died for all, that those who live might no longer live for themselves, but for him who for their sake died and was raised",—2 Corinthians 5:14-15, ESV.

BREATH PRAYER

Teach us to order the steps of our marriage by the love of Christ rather than self-love.

OBJECT STORY

WHO'S IN CONTROL OF YOUR MARRIAGE?

We had the fortune to have our recently married godson, Ryan, and his wife, Amber, visit us from Detroit. We walked with Ryan and Amber through their dating and engagement stages, so it is particularly gratifying to see them start this Christian walk together as 'one flesh.' Ryan and Amber's visit made us think about the early years in our own marriage—over thirty-five years ago. We really wish we had an older mentor couple that directed us. We made so many egregious errors during those days. In a real sense, it is the Easter message that prevented us from doing more serious damage to our relationship. We'd like to offer the words of the Apostle Paul to encourage you to embrace the Easter message in your marriage every single day—not just one weekend a year. It reads as such...

"For the love of Christ controls us, because we have concluded this: that ONE has died for all, therefore all have died; and he died for all, that those who live might no longer live for themselves, but for him who for their sake died and was raised." (2 Corinthians 5:14-15, ESV)

As we break down these two verses, we are inspired. Examine them closely with us because within these verses is the Easter message, "One has died for all." Christ died for all humanity. It was a physical death suffered in the most torturous manner available to the Romans—crucifixion. Upon close examination of the passage you see that Christ died for all in order that all might die. Our death, however, is not a physical death like Jesus'. Rather, it is a death to sin for all that call Jesus Lord. At its core, sin is always an exaggerated and uncompromising love of self. But, Christ's death liberates us from untamed love of self. We know of this sacrifice...but do we really understand why Christ died for all? The Apostle Paul gives us the clue in the very first sentence of the passage.

Prayer Lesson 16
Pray for Selfless Love

2 Corinthians 5:14-15

We have to die to sin so that the love of Christ (rather than the love of self) controls us. The Adversary is a master of self-love (which caused his downfall from God's presence) and he encourages you to let self-love be the downfall of your marriage as well.

This is the ultimate reason Christ died—so that we will no longer live for ourselves. The love of Christ must change the way that you love your spouse. The love of Christ must transform your marriage from good to great. The love of Christ also transforms a selfish self-love to a healthy Christ-like self-love; one that praised the Lord for what He created you to be.

The Lenten/Easter message is not relegated to one season a year. Rather, it is a constant reminder that your life (and your marriage) is not your own. It wholly belongs to Christ because He died for all. Will you let self-love die in your marriage so that Christ's love wields its control? We would like to offer these words to our godson and his wife (words that we wish someone had taught us in our early marriage): God gave everything that was most dear to Him in order that you would live for your spouse and your neighbor. You honor Him every time you do that and you dishonor Him every single time you love yourself more than Christ. This is the greatest commandment. The awesome irony of that is that you are also the benefactor when you love your spouse and others as He has called us to.

Let's talk

MONDAY
- How does the love of Christ control your marriage?
- In what ways in your marriage does the selfish love of self dampen how the love of Christ manifests? Explain.

TUESDAY
- What does Christ's crucifixion mean for your marriage, especially the difficult days?
- What in your marriage must die in order for it to live?

WEDNESDAY
- What most excites you about having a marriage that is lived in a way that brings people to the Lord?
- How would you advise a newlywed couple to practically replace a selfish love of self with the love of Christ?

THURSDAY
- What is one thing that has worked very successfully in your marriage to date but that you need to do differently in order for it to grow?
- What does it mean to you to completely give up your marriage to God?

FRIDAY
- How has your marriage grown since last year?
- Do you believe that you dishonor God every single time you allow sin to disrupt your unity as a couple? How do you feel about that?

Prayer Lesson 16
Pray for Selfless Love

2 Corinthians 5:14-15

Let's Reflect

> Pray for Selfless Love

This week, your reflections and prayers focus on how to model the love of Christ rather than the selfish love of self. Knowing that Christ is privy to every interaction between you as a couple this week, what would most disappoint Him? What would most please him? How do you feel about your responses?

_____

_____

_____

_____

_____

_____

2 Corinthians 5:14-15

Prayer Lesson 16
Pray for Selfless Love

MONDAY

Dear Lord, thank you for the sacrifice that you made for our marriage. You suffered and died in the most heinous way in order that we might have the freedom to live in the fullness of God. You paid for the sins of our marriage so that we had a path away from sinfulness. The presence of the Holy Spirit teaches and encourages us to love like you love. It is the love of Christ that has kept us going and loving in our marriage even when we were struggling to really like each other. Thank you for continuing to pursue us until we were wise enough to understand it for ourselves. Will you continue to extend your grace to us as we aim to control the ways that our love of ourselves gets in the way of what you desire to do in and through us? Show us what is possible in our marriage when we really embody your love. In the name of the Absolute Jesus Christ of Nazareth we pray. Amen.

TUESDAY

Dear Lord, your shed blood is as powerful today as it was over two thousand years ago when you hung on the Roman cross at Golgotha. It's your blood that brought our marriage to the Father's throne. Your blood has pushed our sinful pursuits from the forefront of our imaginations. Your blood keeps us coming back together and working things out when our ego is wounded. Your blood helps us be content when we don't have all of the answers. Your blood keeps us hopeful about who we are even when we are struggling to find our place in the culture around us. Your blood washes over our minds with waves of peace when we feel like darkness is blinding our path ahead. May we always be entreated by your blood towards holiness in who we are, what we know, and what we do. In the name of the Absolute Jesus Christ of Nazareth we pray. Amen.

WEDNESDAY

Dear Lord, our world is filled with sin. Our jobs, neighborhoods, entertainment, and leaders are mired in blatantly sinful behaviors. We know you will not tolerate these sinful behaviors forever. People ignore the biblical precedent for how you turned whole nations over to a reprobate mind because of the hardness of their hearts to the ways of God. But, our marriage is supposed to be a fresh wind that catches the attention of those who are impervious to your will. Our marriage casts a light on the evil that is lurking in the shadows. We rebuke the Adversary and his demons from our circles of influence. We want him to know that we are armed with the banner of the Lord Jesus Christ and we are not afraid of him. We are declaring victory over sin because of the finished work that Christ has already done. In the name of the Absolute Jesus Christ of Nazareth we pray. Amen.

THURSDAY

Dear Lord, the road to the cross is paved with surrender. The only way to get to the cross is to learn to surrender the walk to it. The only way to pick up the cross as you invite us to do is to surrender our will. The only way to follow you with the cross in tow is to surrender its weight to you. And, the only way to be transformed by the cross is to surrender our lives on it just as you did. After three days in the ground, you rose from the grave transformed from mortality to immortality. Our marriage's transformation lies in the walk to the cross, picking up the cross, carrying the cross, and learning to die daily on that same cross. We accept our cross because in it we are discovering all that you meant for us to be from the beginning. In the name of the Absolute Jesus Christ of Nazareth we pray. Amen.

Prayer Lesson 16
Pray for Selfless Love

2 Corinthians 5:14-15

FRIDAY

Dear Lord, we need to ask your forgiveness because we do not believe that you are present with us. If we truly believed you were right here with us, we wouldn't speak with sarcasm, impatience, or deceit. It is shameful for us to admit that the only way that we keep behaving in these sinful ways is that we don't really believe that you are right here. How can we believe that you are everywhere but still not believe that you are right here? How can we believe that you know everything but still not believe that you don't know the hardness of our hearts that allows us to ignore you? It is our simple and shameful confession, Lord, that we ignore you although we claim to serve you. Help us to stop lying to ourselves and each other. We have done much that is wrong, Lord. But, we want to start doing more things right. In the name of the Absolute Jesus Christ of Nazareth we pray. Amen.

PRAY FOR MARITAL WISDOM

REFERENCE SCRIPTURE

"So let us stop going over the basic teachings about Christ again and again. Let us go on instead and become mature in our understanding. Surely we don't need to start again with the fundamental importance of repenting from evil deeds and placing our faith in God.",—Hebrews 6:1, NLT.

BREATH PRAYER

Bless our spiritual eyes that we may see through the lies of the world, the flesh, and the devil.

OBJECT STORY
THE MISEDUCATION OF MARRIAGE

Please read the reference scripture for this lesson again. Biblical scholars posit that the book of Hebrews was written in the latter half of the 1st century to a Jewish community whose faith was faltering because of strong Jewish influences. We must ask ourselves a sobering and rhetorical question: Has anything changed in the twenty centuries since this verse was penned? We as Christian couples are stuck debating about the meaning of the words 'submission' for wives or 'head of the household' for husbands or when we can re-marry if we divorce—we have heard it all before, ad nauseam. Sadly, these and dozens more circular debates set the glass ceiling of our marriages. Hebrews 6:1 admonishes us to stop relishing in this immaturity.

Marriage was designed for us to operate as an elite tactical force, courageously brandishing spiritual weapons for godliness against the forces of evil. Instead, we are a ragtag bunch of modern-day Pharisees who are more interested in our appearance, our rules, our self-righteousness, and our hedonistic pleasure. At the root of our immaturity is our miseducation of marriage.

Most of us have been lying to ourselves ever since 'I do' rolled far too easily off the tongue at the altar. While God designed marriage for our spiritual advancement to produce Kingdom-sanctioned fruit, the sinful culture in which we exist has castrated us and left us unfit for God's work. We have been indoctrinated to believe Christian marriage is primarily about achieving pleasure through companionship, child-bearing, and consumerism/economics—which we label as 'Christian' as long as we credit any gains to the blessings of God and maybe put something in the offering plate.

Prayer Lesson 17
Pray for Marital Wisdom

Hebrews 6:1

We are socialized from our earliest recollection to believe marriage is about control (aggressive or passive) and how to wield it to ensure our happiness. For most of our Christian marriages, the honeymoon bills haven't even been fully paid before the winds of manipulation blow. Disagreements become the norm. Tension is palpable. Arguments intensify. Intimacy wanes. Blaming and distrust leave little room for humility, repentance, or forgiveness. Yet, a facade of happiness (at least a thin one) must be maintained for our Christian circles.

If this toxic sequence describes your marriage in full or in part or you know in your spirit there is a lack of zeal to actively advance your calling as a couple, please know that these circumstances do not truly reflect who you are as a marriage under Christ's umbrella. Only spiritual solutions can rectify spiritual problems. This is why we must embrace the spiritual disciplines as couples. The Holy Spirit is demanding that we grow in our relationship to Christ and as a couple by daily committing ourselves to one or more spiritual disciplines like meditation, fasting, prayer, solitude, worship, study, and simplicity, to name a few.

When you joined together with your spouse under the banner of Christ, the Lord placed within your marriage a priceless treasure—a unique, interwoven spiritual DNA strand only accessible through the spiritual disciplines. Your journey of marriage and its promise is to heed the Apostle Paul's admonition to spend your entire marriage training yourselves and fully exploiting your DNA's abilities as co-workers of the gospel until you die (1 Timothy 4:7). This and only this is the true purpose of Christian marriage. In this service alone will you find the fullness of personal joy you seek.

Let's Talk

MONDAY
- In what ways, if any, have you put a ceiling on how high your marriage can go?
- How, if at all, have you each been miseducated about what a godly marriage requires?

TUESDAY
- If when you got married, you knew what you do now know, what would you have done differently in your first year of marriage?
- If you have unmarried children or hope to have them one day, how would you advise them to select a spouse based on what you have learned?

WEDNESDAY
- The Apostle Paul teaches us the importance of using spiritual rather than earthly weapons. Which earthly weapon(s) do you use most often with your spouse? What is its danger?
- How difficult is it for each of you to give up your use of earthly weapons when you are in a disagreement with your spouse?

THURSDAY
- What spiritual weapons are most natural for you to wield in your marriage?
- How would it feel for your spouse to interrupt your next disagreement with a spiritual weapon? How can you put your mind in the right posture to notice?

FRIDAY
- In what, if any, ways are manipulation and control eroding your marriage? What does this look like?
- What will it take for you each to fully relinquish your willful manipulation and control to God?

PRAYER LESSON 17
Pray for Marital Wisdom

Hebrews 6:1

Let's Reflect

> Pray for Marital Wisdom

Read 2 Corinthian 10:3-5. In the space below, make two columns—one labeled 'earthly weapons' and the other labeled 'spiritual weapons.' In the earthly weapons column, write the words and behaviors you tend to employ when you each are acting without allowing the Holy Spirit to guard your heart, mind, and tongue. Now, in the other column, write the ways in which you are transforming each of the earthly weapons into a spiritual weapon. For example, if you wrote 'withdrawing for extended periods' as an earthly weapon you used, you might write 'staying prayerfully engaged.'

_____

_____

_____

_____

_____

Let's Pray

MONDAY

Dear Lord, you declared that we are "more than conquerors" as we walk in your ways. We've experienced some fulfilling victories in our marriage. But, it's way too easy to think that victories can be achieved in our own strength. It's way too easy for us to take undue credit for the victories. But, to be "more than a conqueror" can be only achieved through your supernatural power. Being "more than a conqueror" refers to those victories that shift our paradigm and make us see things in a different light. Being "more than a conqueror" means there is a new normal—old things are passed away and as a couple we are witnessing an entirely new way of thinking—renewed minds. Lord, help us to break through the internal "ceiling" that has stymied our growth. In the name of the Absolute Jesus Christ of Nazareth we pray. Amen.

TUESDAY

Dear Lord, we've stumbled badly in consistently demonstrating love towards one another, especially in times of distress. When stressors come, we too easily abandon our righteous convictions in favor of blaming and finger pointing. Help us to re-establish a deep-seated friendship in our marriage where we feel trust and security. Help each of us to be worthy of the trust that we desire. Strengthen our dependence on you to pull us towards you as our mutual friend—a base from which we can further our own friendship as a couple. Friendship means a willingness to give and to receive. Despite our past, give us the courage to give generously and receive graciously. In the name of the Absolute Jesus Christ of Nazareth we pray. Amen.

WEDNESDAY

Dear Lord, our instinct when feeling upset with one another is to say or act in unredeemed ways rather than responding with grace and love. In our marriage, our tongues are usually the culprit—saying words and intonations that do not glorify you. Scripture reminds us that we cannot tame the tongue (James 3:8) although we can control it. The Book of James (1:19) teaches us to be "quick to listen, slow to speak, and slow to anger." You have shown us exceeding grace in the filth that has come out our mouths and directed towards each other. We are unworthy of this level of grace, though we are immensely grateful for it. Help us to redeem our tongues so that they are spiritual weapons rather than early ones. In the name of the Absolute Jesus Christ of Nazareth we pray. Amen.

THURSDAY

Dear Lord, spiritual weapons tear down strongholds because they elevate your lordship through Jesus Christ and invoke His power to govern our life circumstances. But, like any physical weapon, we must become weapons experts if we want to masterfully use the spiritual weapon. Weapons mastery takes a lot of practice as we refuse to give in to our flesh in one encounter after another. Through prayer, fasting, and supplication, we call on the power of the Living God to break the chains that bind us and establish a solid foothold on your transforming grace. Show us how to build each other up with these spiritual weapons. Help us embrace these spiritual weapons to deepen our friendship. Make us inconsolable when we willfully stay outside the protection you offer us. In the name of the Absolute Jesus Christ of Nazareth we pray. Amen.

FRIDAY

Dear Lord, the only manipulation and control that we have in our marriage should be our submission to your Holy Spirit to direct us according to your will. We should know better than to keep trying to coerce each other into what we want. We keep trying to push each other into our own image rather than your image. Shamefully, we keep hurting each other in the process. There are ways that we have improved in more quickly recognizing our controlling tendencies. We are grateful for that. We just have to keep pushing those tendencies to the perimeter so that our core stays singly focused on listening to the Holy Spirit's affirmation that our sense of well-being and prosperity come from what you control in our lives rather than what we control. In your control is our contentment. In the name of the Absolute Jesus Christ of Nazareth we pray. Amen.

APPENDIX
INDEX OF PRAYER NEEDS

Marital Challenge	Prayer Lesson Reference Number		
	Volume 1	Volume 2	Volume 3
Accountability	1, 13	24	49
Anxiety/Anxiousness	7	18, 21	46
Blaming	2	22, 26, 34	
Bondage	2	22, 26, 34	
Boredom			37, 45, 47
Christlikeness	12, 13, 16	19, 20	43
Close-minded		24, 28, 29	47
Communication		25, 26, 27, 29	42, 50, 51
Conditional Love	12	20, 23	43, 44, 51, 52
Conflict	10, 15		50
Covenant (Vows)	2, 3	23	50, 51, 52
Creativity			37, 38, 45, 49
Deception	12	20, 30	
Depression		18, 21	
Disbelief	5, 7		39, 40, 43
Discouragement	8	25, 28	35, 49, 50, 51
Disobedience		28	38, 45
Disrespect	3	25	42, 50
Distrust in God / Spouse	4, 7	21, 29	37, 41, 42, 45, 46, 51

Index of Prayer Needs

	Prayer Lesson Reference Number		
Marital Challenge	**Volume 1**	**Volume 2**	**Volume 3**
Listening		25,26	39
Loneliness	9,10	21,22	
Loss / Loss of a	2	19	41
Materialism	17	20	36,40
Mediocrity	3	24,28,30,31	38, 39, 43, 44, 48
Misaligned desires	6,9	25,32	37
Mutual submission	8,9	27	51
Neglect	4	22,26,28,31	42,50
Poor choices	15	21	35
Powerlessness	9,17	18,19,20,22,30	
Prayer gaps	5		39, 43
Pride	1,13		40, 44
Purpose-driven	6,9,16	26,30,33	36, 49, 52
Rejection	10	33	50
Righteousness	13,15	20	40, 48
Risk aversion		34	37, 39
Sanctification	3,14,15,16	23	
Scarcity	5,10	18,20	
Selfishness	8,14,16	20,24,26,29,34	40, 42, 44, 52
Self-limiting beliefs	5	34	47

Appendix

Index of Prayer Needs

Marital Challenge	Prayer Lesson Reference Number		
	Volume 1	Volume 2	Volume 3
Doubt	72	1	42,46
Fear	7	21	35,41
Fighting		29	48.50
Financial Difficulties		26	42,50
Gracelessness		26,32	44
Grieving		19	41
Hopelessness	5		44,45
Identity issues			36,40,47
Impatience	10	27,31,35	
Imposter Syndrome	11	20	44
Inattention (to detail)	8	25,27,28,31,32	42
Inconsistency	6	32,35	44
Independence	9	34	42,43
Inflexibility	17	28,31	35
Ingratitude		19,33	45,50
Insecurity		29,33	42,44
Joyless	7,11	18,21,22	
Lack of direction		30	36,39
Lack of intimacy /romance	9	22,25,33	37,42,45,50,51
Lack of vision	6	24	39,49

Index of Prayer Needs

	Prayer Lesson Reference Number		
Marital Challenge	**Volume 1**	**Volume 2**	**Volume 3**
Self-reliance	1, 4, 16	30	
Self-righteousness	3, 15, 17	28	48
Self-worship	4, 12, 15	30	39
Service	8	26	52
Spiritual discipline	1, 11, 13, 17		
Spiritual maturity	1, 2, 4, 12, 13, 17	18, 20	35, 36, 39, 40, 43, 49
Spiritual warfare	2, 5, 12, 15	30	39
Stewardship	3, 8	22, 26	37, 50
Suffering	2	18, 19, 21	41, 46
Superficiality	3	20, 24	
Surrender	14, 15	19, 28	
Togetherness	9,	24, 27, 28	
Trials	2, 5	18, 21	46
Unanswered prayers	2	20, 22, 24	
Uncontrolled thoughts	7, 11	21	
Undisciplined	6, 8	26	35
Unhappy		22	38, 45, 51
Untapped potential	5, 6	24, 32, 33	43
Worldliness	3, 12, 13, 15	20	38, 40, 48

ABOUT THE AUTHORS

Dr. Harold (Psychologist) and Dalia W. Arnold (CPA) have committed their marriage of more than thirty-five years to help everyday couples discover the spiritual power Christian marriage holds to transform them into dynamic intercessors for the Kingdom of God at home and beyond. Together, the Arnolds serve as founders of the national non-profit marriage organization, Eusebeia (www.prayformarriage.com), a ministry promoting spiritual intimacy in Christian marriage, as well as marriage ministers in the local church. Dr. Harold's books include *The Unfair Advantage, Marriage ROCKS for Christian Couples,* and *Second Shift.* The Arnolds reside in the Philadelphia metropolitan area and are grateful parents of two amazingly creative adult children.

The Arnolds are both graduates of Howard University's Business School in Computer Information Systems (Harold) and Accounting (Dalia). Dr. Harold went on to pursue graduate studies in Systems Engineering (University of MD, College Park), Marriage and Family Therapy (Fuller Theological Seminary), and Psychology (Temple University). Dalia earned her CPA and Certification in Biblical Counseling (Christian Research & Development Training Institute). The Arnolds are currently pursing certification in spiritual direction with a focus on spiritual formation in marriage.

www.ingramcontent.com/pod-product-compliance
Lightning Source LLC
LaVergne TN
LVHW020931090426
835512LV00020B/3312